RIGHT AND LEFT

Joseph Roth (1894–1939) was the great elegist of the cosmopolitan, tolerant and doomed Central European culture that flourished in the dying days of the Austrian Empire. His books include *The Legend of the Holy Drinker*, *Confession of a Murderer*, *Flight Without End*, *The String of Pearls*, *The Silent Prophet*, *The Emperor's Tomb*, *Hotel Savoy*, *Tarabas* and *The Radetzky March*.

Michael Hofmann is a poet. His most recent collection is *Approximately Nowhere*. As a translator his work includes Franz Kafka's *The Man Who Disappeared (Amerika)*. He has also translated Roth's *The Legend of the Holy Drinker*, *The String of Pearls* and *Rebellion*.

RIGHT AND LEFT

Joseph Roth

Translated from the German
by Michael Hofmann

Granta Books
London

Granta Publications, 2/3 Hanover Yard, London N1 8BE

First published in Great Britain by Chatto & Windus 1991
This edition published by Granta Books 1999

Original title *Rechts und Links* by Joseph Roth. First published
1929.

A CIP catalogue record for this book
is available from the British Library.

3 5 7 9 10 8 6 4 2

Typeset by M Rules
Printed and bound in Great Britain by Mackays of Chatham plc

Part One

1

I can still remember the time when Paul Bernheim promised to be a genius.

He was the grandson of a horse-trader who had saved up a small fortune, and the son of a banker who had forgotten how to save, but on whom fortune had smiled. Paul's father, Herr Felix Bernheim, went arrogantly through life, and had many enemies, although a normal measure of foolishness would have been enough to secure him the esteem of his fellow citizens. Instead, his exceptional good fortune aroused their envy. Then one day, as though fate intended to reduce them to complete despair, it presented him with a jackpot.

Most people would keep such a thing as secret as a stain on the family honour. Herr Bernheim, however, perhaps afraid that his good fortune would not provoke a sufficiently furious response, now redoubled his palpable contempt for the world at large, further reduced the number of greetings he would give in the course of a day – which was small already – and began to answer the greetings of others with a casual and offensive show of absent-mindedness. Not content with which, having so far only provoked his fellow men, he now set about provoking nature. He lived in the large house his father had built just outside town, on the road that led to the forest. The house was set in an old garden, among fruit trees, oaks and limes. It was painted yellow, had a steep red roof, and was surrounded by a high grey wall. The trees round the edge of the garden grew over the wall and their branches spread over the road. For many years past, two wide green benches had stood by the wall for the tired traveller to rest on. Swallows nested in the house, and the crowns of the trees were a-twitter in the summer evenings. The long wall, the trees and the benches were a source of cool and shade in the heat and dust of summer, and on bitter winter days they were at least an intimation of a human presence.

One summer day, the green benches disappeared. Wooden scaffolding went up, topping the wall. In the garden, the old trees were felled. One could hear them splinter and crash, and hear the death-rustling of their branches as they hit the ground. The wall came down. And through the gaps in the wooden scaffolding, people could see the denuded garden of the Bernheims, the yellow house now exposed to the scorching heat, and they were as indignant as if the house, the wall and the trees had all been theirs.

A few months later, the old yellow gabled house was replaced by a gleaming new white one, which had a stone balcony shouldered by a plaster Atlas, a flat roof of southern inspiration, modish ornamentation between the windows, little cherubs' heads and grimacing devils alternating along the frieze, and an imposing approach which might have graced a supreme court, a parliament or a university. Instead of the stone wall, a tight-meshed steel fence raised its sharpened points against the heavens, the

4

birds and burglars. In the garden were boring round or heart-shaped flowerbeds, artificial lawns of short, dense, almost blue grass, and frail rose trees teetering on wooden trellises. Set among the flowerbeds were clay gnomes, with red caps, smiling faces and white beards, holding spades, hammers and watering cans in their tiny hands, a whole fairytale population courtesy of Grützer & Co. Artfully winding gravel paths snaked round the flowerbeds, crunchy even to the eye. Not a bench was to be seen. And although one was merely standing outside, one's legs grew tired from the sight of so much busy magnificence, as though one had walked about in it for hours. The gnomes grinned in vain. The frail rose trees teetered, the pansies looked like painted china. And even when the gardener's long hose scattered little droplets of water, one felt no refreshment. Rather, one was reminded of the sweet and scented liquids that the usher sprinkles on the bare heads of cinema-goers. Over the balcony, Herr Bernheim put up the words *Sans Souci* in jagged gold lettering that was difficult to read.

In the afternoons Herr Bernheim could be seen walking about his flowerbeds with the gardener, raping nature. One could hear the hissing bite of the shears, and the crashing of the low hedges, newly planted and only just beginning to grow, when they became acquainted with the conditions of their service. The windows of the house were never open, and usually the curtains were drawn too. On some evenings the silhouettes could be discerned, through the thick yellow curtains, of people walking and sitting, the clustered radiance of a chandelier, and one guessed there was a party at the Bernheims'.

There was a certain cool dignity about these parties. The wine that was drunk in that house failed in its purpose, though it was of select vintage. One drank it and became sober. Herr Bernheim's guests were local landowners, some military men with the right feudal touch, and a few very carefully chosen representatives of industry and commerce. Awe of them, and fear of losing his dignity, kept Herr Bernheim from enjoying himself. His guests, sensing their host's unease, remained all evening what they had been on their arrival, which is to say, *comme il faut*. Frau Bernheim missed the point of jokes and found anecdotes unamusing. She was, incidentally, of Jewish descent – and as the majority of the jokes that circulated among her guests began with the words: 'There was once a Jew on a train . . .', Frau Bernheim would feel offended as well as puzzled, and as soon as someone seemed to be about to tell a joke, she would fall into a gloomy and confused silence – afraid lest Jews should be mentioned. Herr Bernheim thought it unfitting to talk shop with his guests, who in turn considered it unnecessary to talk to him about agriculture, the army or horseflesh. Sometimes Bertha, the only daughter of the house, and a good match, would play Chopin with just the degree of virtuosity to be expected from a well brought-up young lady. Sometimes there would be dancing. And at one o'clock the guests would go home. The lights would go out in the windows. Everyone slept. Only the nightwatchman, the dog and the gnomes in the garden remained awake.

As was customary in houses with well-run nurseries, Paul Bernheim went to bed at nine o'clock. He shared a room with his younger brother Theodor. Paul would stay awake. He could only sleep when the whole house was quiet. He was a sensitive boy. They called him 'a nervous child', and his sensitivity seemed to indicate exceptional talents.

In his early years, he was at pains to display these. Paul was twelve when the Bernheims hit their jackpot, but he had the understanding of an eighteen-year-old. The rapid transformation from solid middle class to wealth with feudal aspirations fuelled his own innate ambition. He knew that a father's wealth or social standing can help his son to a powerful 'position'. He imitated his father's arrogance. He took on his classmates and teachers. He had broad hips, languid movements, a full, red, half-open mouth with short white teeth, a pale, greenish complexion, sparkling empty eyes with long, black lashes and long, provocative, silken hair. He sat at his desk, absent-minded, casual and smiling. His posture betrayed the thought constantly going through his mind: My father could buy this place. His classmates were small and helpless, at the mercy of the school's authority. He alone opposed it with the power of his father, his room, his English breakfast of ham and eggs and orange segments, his private tutor, whose lessons he imbibed with the aid of hot chocolate and biscuits every afternoon, his wine-cellar, his car, his garden and his gnomes. He gave off a smell of milk, warmth, soap, baths, gymnastic exercises, doctors' calls and housemaids. It was as though school and homework took up only an insignificant part of his day. He already had one foot in the bigger world outside. The voices of his classmates echoing in his ear, he sat in the classroom like a visitor. He never altogether belonged.

Sometimes his father would come to pick him up in the car, an hour early. The following day, Paul would have a note from the doctor.

He sometimes appeared lonely, but it was not possible for him to make friends. His wealth forever stood between him and the others. 'Come over in the afternoon when my tutor's there – then he can do our prep for us,' he would say. But it was rare for anyone ever to take him up. All the emphasis was on 'my tutor'.

He learned with facility and his guesswork was good. He read a lot. His father had provided him with a library. He would sometimes say, when it wasn't strictly necessary, 'my son's library', or, to the maid: 'Anna, go to my son's library!' – although it was the only one in the house. One day Paul attempted a drawing of his father from a photograph. 'My son is astonishingly gifted,' said old Bernheim – and he bought sketchbooks, pastels, canvases, brushes and oil paints, engaged a drawing tutor, and had part of the attic converted into a studio.

Twice a week, from five till seven, Paul would practise at the piano with his sister. Going past the house, one heard them playing duets – always Tchaikovsky. Sometimes someone would say to him the following day: 'I heard you playing a duet yesterday!' 'Yes, with my sister. She's an even better player than I am!' And how that little word 'even' would irritate them!

His parents took him to concerts. He would hum melodies, list works, composers, concert halls, the conductors he loved to imitate. In the summer holidays he would always go away somewhere – taking his tutor with him, lest 'his work suffered'. He would go up to the mountains, cross the seas to strange shores, and return proudly and silently, contenting himself with arrogant hints, as though he took it for granted that the others were just as well-travelled as he was. He was experienced. He had already seen everything he read and heard about. His quick brain made clever connections. His library provided him with unnecessary details to impress with. His list of 'private reading' was the most extensive of anyone's. His offhand manner was forgiven. It cast no blemish on his 'moral conduct'. A background like Bernheim's was in itself a sufficient guarantee of ethical behaviour. Awkward teachers would be brought to heel by Bernheim senior, with invitations to a 'modest supper'. They would return to their spartan dwellings intimidated by the sight of the parquet, the pictures, the servants and the pretty daughter.

Paul Bernheim was far from ill at ease with girls. In time he became a good dancer, an agreeable conversationalist, a well-trained sportsman. Over the months and years his enthusiasms and talents changed. For six months he was passionate about music, for a month it was fencing, for a year drawing, for another year literature, then finally it was the young wife of a magistrate, whose demand for young men could hardly be satisfied in what was only a middle-sized town. All his talents and passions came together in his love for her. He would paint rural scenes, fence, compose, write odes to nature, all for her. Finally she turned her attentions to a cadet, and Paul immersed himself in art history, 'to forget'. This was now where he placed all his devotion. Soon he was unable to see a human being, a road, a bit of field, without referring to some well-known painting by a famous master. Though still young, he outdid even the most highly-regarded art historians in his inability to see an object directly and describe it in simple terms.

But this passion also faded. It made way for social ambition. Perhaps it had only existed as a form of preparation for it, being the ideal scientific underpinning for a socialite's career. It was possible that Paul Bernheim had taken his blissfully naive, charming and inquisitive upward gaze from certain devotional paintings. This gaze was half-directed at man yet brushed the heavens. Through their long lashes, Paul's eyes seemed to filter a heavenly illumination.

Equipped with such charms, and with his tastes informed by art and learned commentaries, he plunged into the social life of the town, which mainly consisted of the efforts of mothers to find matches for their marriageable daughters. Paul was a welcome guest in any house where such girls lived. He could strike whatever note was required. He was like a musician able to play all the instruments in the orchestra, and play them badly but charmingly. He could spout wisely (things he'd read or thought) by the hour. An hour later, he would be all warm, smiling chattiness, producing a feeble anecdote for the tenth time, newly embroidered on each occasion; caressing some banal aphorism with his tongue, gripping it between his teeth for a while and tasting it with his lips; producing someone else's successful witticism with an easy conscience; making quite shameless fun of absent acquaintances. And the girls would giggle, giggle nakedly. They would only be baring their teeth, but it was as though they were baring their young breasts; they would only clap their hands, but it was as though they were opening their legs; they would show him their books and pictures and sheet music, but it was as though they were pulling back the sheets; they put up their hair, but it was as though they were loosing it. It was at this time that Paul started visiting the brothel twice a week, with the regularity of an elderly civil servant, and he described to his friends the charms of imaginary girls, whom of course he compared to celebrated paintings. He gave away the secrets of this or that daughter of the house, and described the breasts he claimed to have seen and felt.

He was still painting, drawing, composing and writing. When his sister became engaged – to a cavalry captain, by the way – he wrote a long poem for the occasion, which he set to music and sang to his own accompaniment. Later – his brother-in-law was mechanically minded – Paul took an interest in machines, and started to take apart the engine of his car – one of the first to appear in the town. Finally he took riding lessons so as to be able to keep his brother-in-law company on rides in the little pinewood. The inhabitants of the town, recognising that old Herr Bernheim had presented his home town with a genius, softened in their attitude towards him. Quite a few of Bernheim's enemies, having felt offended for a long time, now, with daughters growing up in their families, began to greet Felix Bernheim once more.

At that time there was a rumour that Herr Bernheim was about to receive some great distinction. There was talk of his elevation to the ranks of the nobility. It was instructive to observe how the prospect of Bernheim's ennoblement soothed the virulence of his opponents. The future nobility of Bernheim was a perfectly satisfactory explanation for the arrogance of his present bourgeois self. The scientific basis for his pride had been discovered, and it was found to be quite acceptable. For, in the opinion of the town, arrogance might fittingly grace the noble, the ennobled, and even the shortly-to-be-ennobled.

What actual basis this rumour may have had is unknown. Perhaps Herr Bernheim would only have been made a commercial counsellor. But then something unexpected happened, something improbable. A story so banal one would be ashamed to tell it in a novel, for instance.

One day a travelling circus came to town. During the tenth or eleventh performance there was an accident: a young female acrobat fell from her trapeze, right into the box where Herr Felix Bernheim was sitting – on his own (his family considered circuses to be a vulgar spectacle). Later it was said that 'with great presence of mind' Herr Bernheim had caught the artiste in his arms. But that cannot be established with any degree of certainty – any more than another rumour, according to which he had been watching the girl since the very first performance, and had been sending her flowers. What is certain is that he conveyed her to hospital, visited her there, and didn't permit her to leave with the rest of the circus. He took an apartment for her, and had the courage to fall in love with her. He, the pride of the bourgeoisie, the rising nobleman, the father-in-law of a cavalry captain, fell in love with a circus tumbler. Frau Bernheim told her husband: 'Bring your mistress home if you like, I'm going to my sister's.'

And she did. The cavalry captain arranged for a transfer to another barracks. Only the two sons and the servants continued to live in the Bernheims' house. The yellow curtains remained drawn for months. But old Bernheim didn't change his ways. He remained arrogant, he defied the whole world, he was in love with the girl. There was no more talk of ennoblement.

It was perhaps the one courageous act of Felix Bernheim's life. Later on, when his son Paul might have undertaken a similar one, I thought of his father's, and from that single example I understood how courage exhausts itself over the generations, and how much feebler are the sons than their fathers.

The girl only stayed in the town for a few months. As though she had only fallen from Heaven for the specific purpose of eliciting an act of courage from Felix Bernheim in the last years of his life, of showing him a fleeting glimmer of beauty, and of bringing about his elevation into the ranks of a natural nobility. One day the girl vanished. Perhaps – if one wanted the romantic story to have a romantic conclusion – perhaps the circus came back to the area, and the girl found that she missed her trapeze. Even acrobatics can be a vocation.

Frau Bernheim returned. The house revived a little. Paul, who had been saddened by his father's adventure, because it had cost him his expected title and because the cavalry captain had left, was quick to recover, and even took pleasure in the fact that his 'old man was really a bit of a lad'.

Otherwise he was preparing for his departure.

He was shortly to begin a new life.

2

He passed his final school exams with predictably excellent marks. From then on he took to wearing new suits. His old schoolboy things seemed unhealthy to him, like clothes worn during a long illness. The new suits were light and loose-fitting, of indeterminate colour, soft and hairy and warm. The material came from England, the country to which Paul Bernheim was intending to go.

None of his contemporaries was going to England. One, who expressed the vague intention of 'improving his French' in Paris, was viewed with suspicion by the rest. But old Bernheim had once said at a party: 'The moment my son's finished school, I'll send him out into the world!' And, for a certain section of the prosperous middle class, the world was England.

These gentlemen had been ordering their suits from England for some years now. They belonged to navy clubs, they praised the British system of government and the British constitution, they met King Edward VII often and as though by chance on the promenade at Marienbad, they did business with Englishmen, they drank whisky and port, although they preferred the taste of Pilsener beer, they formed clubs although they would rather have met at the café, they feigned taciturnity

14

although they were naturally garrulous, they started collections of various useless objects, because they had the idea that a 'gentleman' must needs have a hobby, they did gymnastics in the mornings, spent their summers on the coast to acquire complexions ruddied by the wind and sea air, and told stories about the London pea-soupers, the London Stock Exchange and the London bobbies. Some went so far as to affect 'indeed' instead of 'ja', and to take out subscriptions to English newspapers, which arrived far too late for their contents to be newsworthy. But the subscribers would refuse to acknowledge events if they hadn't read about them in English. 'Let's wait and see,' they would say when something happened. 'The newspaper's due tomorrow.' Their children grew up speaking both English and German. For a time it looked as though there was a little Anglo-Saxon enclave growing up in the town, perhaps ultimately seeking absorption into the British Empire. In this town, with its thoroughly Continental character, where there was never a hint of fog, they had to eat, drink and be clothed as though they were on the roaring sea-coasts of England.

After Paul had been wearing his English suits for a couple of weeks, he announced that he would like to spend a few years in England. And, no doubt afraid that people would fail to appreciate the full value of living and studying in England, he explained: 'It's not as easy as you think, getting into an English college. A foreigner needs recommendations from two Englishmen of standing, otherwise he hasn't a hope! And above all you have to have impeccable manners, which unfortunately is not often the case here! I'm going to Oxford! All next week I'm practising swimming!'

It was as though his plan was to swim to Oxford.

Since he thought of the English as a rather down-to-earth people, he saw little point in studying art history there, and decided instead on a course of history, politics and law. There was no more talk of artists and paintings. In a trice, all the new books he required were in his library. He already had a good idea of Oxford from the prospectuses. He told stories about it, not as one just about to go there, but as though he were already familiar with it. More remarkable, though, than the fact that he discussed the various colleges with the authority of a seasoned observer, was the interest and the credulity of the people who asked him about them. And not only he, but his father also talked about studying at Oxford, and all the members of the clubs that Bernheim senior belonged to also quoted from the Oxford curriculum. And all the girls of marriageable age told each other: 'Paul's going to Oxford!' They referred to him as Paul, as all the middle class of the town did. He was their darling. It is the fate of attractive men everywhere to have strangers refer to them by their Christian names.

Paul set off for Oxford one fine June day, escorted to the station by a few young ladies. His parents had left town the week before to go on their summer holiday, because Paul's mother had declared: 'I don't want to feel left behind if Paul is going away from us for such a long time! It will make it easier for me if I go away too.' Paul was wearing one of his indeterminately coloured suits, he had a pipe jammed in the corner of his mouth, and he

16

stood at the window of his compartment like a figure in a fashion magazine. As the train rolled out of the station, with wonderful dexterity he threw each of the three prettiest girls a rose. Only one of them fell to the ground. The girl bent down to pick it up, and when she looked up again Paul was already out of sight. He was gone, and that still summer evening the whole town felt sad.

At intervals, various persons received letters from Paul Bernheim. They were model letters. The letters of a gentleman. Across thrice-folded paper as thick as parchment, with Paul's monogram embossed in the top left-hand corner in navy blue, marched the broad Roman script, a little spoilt, a little affected, the words well spaced and the margins generously wide. The sender never wrote his name on the envelope. He stamped his monogram on it, in navy blue sealing-wax, a P lodged artfully in the belly of a B, like an embryo in the womb. The tone of these letters of Paul's was strictly conventional. Sporting expressions and bewilderingly alien terms for rowing and sailing boats alternated with the names of distinguished families, while the short, monosyllabic names of his friends, 'Bob', 'Ted' and 'Pete' went off like bangers in the text.

One day he went to the Consulate doctor in London to enlist in the army, obtaining a few years' postponement. Naturally, he was put down for the cavalry.

He communicated these events as follows:

'Well, old chap, the time's come! Cavalry, dragoons with any luck. Telegraphed the old man right away. Two years' grace, by then my riding should be up to snuff for the Wild West. Bought a horse over here, call him

17

Kentucky, licks my face, as much character as a tomcat. Medic was a brick. But then I was the fittest fellow there, some feat, all the rest were pen-pushers, one labourer. Poor specimens. Still, all taken. As though there was a war on. Then spent two days in London, touring the dives. Saw the female sex again, after the monkish life in college. Thought of the old catechist, what a terrific chap he was. He alive still? Well, old boy, another year, and I'll be home for a fortnight. Got to go out now, practise for next week. Big day! Fencing tournament, with ball to follow. Completely forgotten how to dance, will have to learn again from basics. You see, all go. Oh well, cheerio!'

His letters home were no different. He never seemed to have anything particular to communicate, it was as if his correspondence was forced on him by the college time-table, which included writing to one's loved ones back home as well as rowing and fencing.

'What I want to know,' muttered old Bernheim in his club, 'is when those rascals ever get around to doing any work! He never mentions studying.'

The manufacturer Lang, who had the 'closest ties' with England, would not allow the varsity's teaching methods to be called into question like this, and he said, not without a quiver of indignation: 'The English know what's what! Just take a look at them, they know a darn sight more than we do. A healthy mind in a healthy body, that's the idea, what!'

Whereupon four or five gentlemen cried out: '*Mens sana in corpore sano*' all at once and with such vehemence that only one of them was able actually to finish the

18

tag. Herr Lang, who regretted not having produced the classical *bon mot* in its original form himself, hastened to rap his cards down on the table, and, for the first time in many years, cried out: '*Alea jacta est*!' This to establish that all men of Anglo-Saxon persuasion were also humanists to their fingertips.

And they went back to their cards.

This may be an opportune moment to assure readers that, a mere fortnight after the trapeze artiste's disappearance, the amorous adventure of old Herr Bernheim was forgotten as though it had never been. It was a positive feat of amnesia, given the still considerable number of those envious or resentful of Felix Bernheim. One might almost be tempted to conclude that people are uncomfortable when one of their leading lights – even an unpopular one – runs the risk of humiliating himself. In effect, the episode had no lasting consequences, save the transfer of the son-in-law and the daughter's move away. Frau Bernheim was long since installed back in her rightful home. Perhaps in her heart of hearts she still bore a little resentment towards her husband. But she behaved, people said, 'in an exemplary way' and let none of it show. She had a limited intelligence, albeit one that functioned very well within its limits. However, she was a little inclined to over-estimate it. She would proffer opinions on a minister, a poet, the Renaissance, religion – and all in the same condescending tone she used with her servants. On occasions, her pampered voice would utter little idiocies that one would have found forgivable, even charming, if only she'd been thirty years younger. It was as though her pretty and forceful mouth had so long delighted all the world with its

19

inanities that its possessor gradually came to believe that they themselves were charming. She forgot that in the meantime she had become an old woman. She forgot it to the extent that, in spite of her grey hair, which she had now taken to dyeing, in the moment when she said a foolish sentence the old, girlish glow returned to her fallen features, as though conjured up by her forgetfulness, and for just an instant one saw the lovely shadow of her youth flitting across her face. But the shadow disappeared quickly, whereas the folly echoed lingeringly round the room, and the consternation of those who heard it remained, and was even intensified when Herr Bernheim made a vain attempt to save the situation with some tasteless joke.

For how many years now he'd been subjected to these embarrassments! He alone among those present under-stood the terrible difference between the naive phrase born on his wife's once rosy mouth, and that same phrase on her now pallid lips. It frightened him, and he cracked a joke, reflexively, as a man cries out when he's startled. But Frau Bernheim would become 'indignant' on such occasions. She pouted, as she had so success-fully done in her youth, and as a result she suddenly looked another ten years older. She believed she had every right to hold wise opinions. She was certain that 'culture' – which she held in very high regard – was not only a preserve of the upper classes, but was her own birthright too, and that to be able to discourse upon cultural subjects it was enough to have a wealthy hus-band and a son with 'a library' of his own.

She had once been a beauty, and pampered. In her

broad, chiselled face – she had the same hair and complexion as her son Paul – there was an imperturbable calm: the cold, prohibitive calm of a locked gate, rather than that of a vast, deserted landscape. There were no lines of worry on her face, which seemed to treat even the wrinkles of age as unbidden guests, an insulting presence. Her clear grey coquettish eyes had an expression that was at once pleading and hostile. One might have thought of this look as 'majestic' – which was her own estimation of it – if it didn't so obviously disclose the objects over which it held sway: curtains and clothes, rings and necklaces, so-called '*intérieurs*', and household things. Yes, household things. For in addition to her aspiration to live 'like royalty', and to cut a 'majestic figure', she also wanted to be a 'prudent housewife'. When she was putting some superfluous stitches of embroidery on some superfluous cushion-covers in the weeks before Christmas, as 'a surprise' for someone, she would be convinced that she was offering up a sacrifice to the great god Thrift, and it caused her a sweet pang that was almost as enjoyable as tears. 'Look at this, Felix,' she would say, 'I'm sure Frau Lang wouldn't make that for herself.'

'You don't have to make it either,' would come Felix's reply.

'Well, who will then? Do you want to pay a fortune for it?'

'I can do perfectly well without it.'

'You may say that, but if it wasn't there you'd be sorry!'

'You should check the buttons on my overcoat instead – one of them came off today.'

21

'Give it to me!' Frau Bernheim would then say blissfully. 'There's just no relying on Lise, is there! I have to do everything myself!'

And with the cheerful sigh that makes a task appear harder and more valuable, and thereby flatters the self-esteem of the toiler, Frau Bernheim began to sew on the button.

'Paul tells me in his letters,' she began again, 'that you don't give him enough money.'

'I know what I'm doing!'

'Yes, but you don't know Oxford!'

'You don't know it any more than I do.'

'Oh?! And wasn't cousin Fritz at the Sorbonne?'

'That's completely different, and anyway, so what?'

'Felix, please, don't be rude!' And Felix thought about whether he might perhaps have been rude. He said nothing more. After all, Frau Bernheim had 'forgotten' the whole thing already.

'There, now that button will hold forever!' she said with childish joy.

And they went to bed.

There was rarely any mention made of Theodor, their younger son. As he took after his father more than his mother – or at least so Frau Bernheim would say at every opportunity – he was not thought to be 'a genius' like his brother. For Frau Bernheim thought of her husband as simply lucky. She didn't believe he actually knew anything, nor did she think him capable of learning. She had the contempt for commerce and businessmen that some daughters of upper-middle class families in the nineties acquired with their education, along with their dowry,

22

belles-lettres and playing the piano. In Frau Bernheim's estimation, a civil servant ranked higher than a banker, and a financier was incapable of acquiring 'culture'. As she had a cousin who was a barrister, her marriage was forever a misalliance in her eyes. In her younger years, she had sometimes thought of deceiving her husband with an officer or a professor. Sexual intercourse with a social superior might have lent piquancy to her lavishing herself on a mere banker. If one heard Frau Bernheim, who was, of course 'prey to her nerves', shout 'Oh Felix!' or complain about the 'noisy house' when the wind slammed a door or window shut, or say 'Oh do watch where you're going!' when her husband happened to knock over a chair, then one could detect the monstrous injury that fortune had dealt her.

And yet she was often able to give her husband surprisingly good advice, to see financial perils looming, to sense the ill will of certain parties, to maintain a shrewd mistrust of servants, bills and tradesmen, to keep order in her household, to organise summer holidays, and to gain the respect of porters, naval officers and hotel staff. She was possessed of an animal instinct for home and family, and this was the source of her caution, her cleverness, and her kindness too, although this last stopped abruptly at the garden fence.

Outside it, her toughness, her implacability, her deafness and blindness prevailed. She drew a distinction between those poor people who had somehow gained access to her house, and the others who had to beg in the streets. And she could organise her charity to the extent that her heart needed to function only at certain hours of certain days. To do good, at intervals and within limits, was imperative to her. But if, for example, one were to tell her about some calamity that had befallen a family she didn't know, her interest would confine itself to the details of the case, whether it had occurred on a Wednesday or a Thursday, by day or at night, indoors or out of doors. Thereafter, for all her curiosity as to the exact circumstances of the misfortune, nothing could have induced her to approach its victims. She avoided the sites of illness and mishap, cemeteries and sickrooms. She had an idea that such places might be infectious. If her husband came to her and said: 'Lang or Stauffer or Frau Wagram is unwell,' her reply would be: 'Then mind you don't go there, Felix!' All forms of fanaticism are cruel. Fanatical valetudinarianism is no exception.

She missed her son Paul. She read his brisk letters several times over, never understood them, and tried to find out, by reading between the lines, whether 'her boy' was well, or was perhaps keeping quiet about some illness. She thought of him as a 'dear child' who suffered in silence. She wrote to him twice a week – not replies to his letters, not communications of her own, but words and syllables to take the place of kisses and embraces, to create a physical contact. Paul would skim over these letters and then burn them. He was displeased with his mother. He would have preferred a real lady as a mother, and it was as such that he described her to strangers. Sometimes he would dream of educating her. He imagined living with her on an English country estate. She would have white hair, read Thomas Hardy novels, and enjoy the respect of the local aristocracy. In his accounts, she took on the form, the quality, the character and the significance she liked to accord herself. Equally, when he spoke about his father, he would produce a mild caricature of him, rather as she did. But then, he rarely spoke of his country and his home, because he couldn't tell the truth about them, and he lacked the confidence to lie.

He was planning to remain in England for another year and a half at least. But one day he received a telegram calling him home.

A week earlier, old Herr Bernheim had set off on a long voyage. He had wanted to go to Egypt for his gout. But almost as soon as he boarded the steamer at Marseilles he died. He was in the company of a young woman whom he had passed off as his daughter, and who was perhaps – who can say – a contributory cause of his unexpected death. When his body was returned for burial, there was no money about his person. Some accounts had it that the girl was the acrobat. But people are inclined to put a novelettish construction on the simplest events. What is more probable is that the man had a fondness for girls in general, and that his commitment to a particular one, and a conveniently elusive one at that, was probably a figment of the imagination. Even so, his death on board ship, at the sea's edge, and in the arms of what one hopes was a beautiful girl, had more freedom and dignity about it than most of his life, or at least what we know of his life. Because it is possible that Herr Felix Bernheim led an existence that was never entirely straightforward. It is possible that he really was, as his son Paul called him, 'a bit of a lad', rough, healthy, happy and easygoing.

His son-in-law, the cavalry captain, went to collect the body. Paul attended the funeral.

At the graveside Frau Bernheim wept, surrounded by her children. Her beautiful, cold eyes were red, like chips of glittering, bloodied ice. Herr Bernheim was buried in a marble mausoleum. On the wide, blue-veined slab was a summary of what he had accomplished in life, in plain black lettering more dignified than the 'Sans Souci' he had had put up over his villa. But as for the grieving angel leaning over the cross, he remains a brother of the little cherubs that ornament the frieze of the Bernheims' house.

3

Gradually, Paul became more Continental again. It seemed to go with the sombre and dignified clothes he wore during the mourning period for his father. For the moment, there could be no question of his returning to England. He had little idea about business. He wasn't sure whether he should go into the bank, or resume his studies; nor yet what he ought to study. His father had left three different wills, none of them particularly recent. There was a whisper of things being amiss in the Bernheim house and bank – a suggestion that their fortune was considerably smaller than had been thought.

Paul could say nothing definite about his future plans. He was still talking about the varsity, but the things he was saying were no different from when he had only read about it in the prospectuses. He spent hours in his father's office, poring desultorily over the books, talking to secretaries and old bank officials, permanently on guard lest his inexperience be found out and exploited by them. Something of his mother's suspicious nature, something of her frosty stubbornness began to appear in Paul. He too would never admit to his ignorance of something to an elderly employee, say. And then he had to fend off his mother's advice, and that of one of her brothers, with whom old Bernheim senior had been forever crossing swords, and who had now reappeared on the scene.

Such was Paul's predicament when the war came to his rescue. From the outset he was passionate for Fatherland, horses and the dragoons. Frau Bernheim, convinced that death only came for the poor infantryman, once more had occasion to be proud of her son. When he stood before her in uniform for the first time – he enlisted in full regalia, in spite of never having been a soldier before – she wept: firstly, with joy at how handsome he looked; then, because her husband was no longer alive to witness the moment; and thirdly, because the sight of a uniform never failed to move her. (This last could be traced back to her girlhood days.)

In accordance with the regimental traditions of the dragoons – though these had become relaxed with time, and especially with the outbreak of war – Paul grew a little toothbrush moustache. He looked more soldierly than the other one-year volunteers. His horsemanship, his patriotism and his uniform would have convinced most observers that Paul Bernheim was the scion of an old cavalry family. He tried by his enthusiasm to make up for his low birth. He also took to signing his name so airily that it might as easily have been 'von Bernheim' as plain 'Bernheim'.

But then, as the result of an edict that appalled him quite as much as some of his contemporaries were appalled by their call-up, he was forced to quit the cavalry. By its prejudices, the state lost an excellent officer, perhaps even a hero in the making. For there can be no doubt that Paul Bernheim's vanity would have

28

expressed itself in patriotic heroism. But the terms of the edict turned him into a quartermaster.

How many would have changed places with him! But he, in almost the same hour as he left the dragoons, turned into an embittered pacifist. A new path to a meaningful destiny opened up before him. He got in touch with opponents of the war, he wrote for small, banned, dissident journals and addressed secret pacifist meetings. And although he was neither a good journalist nor a good speaker, he caught the imagination of the little people, private soldiers, deserters and revolutionaries, thanks to his officer's rank, his polished appearance, his evidently solid background. The sheen of his insignia, the jingle of his spurs – because even as a quartermaster, he continued to be mounted – his delicate olive complexion, the lissom movements of his arms and hips fascinated them; and since he had donated the measure of heroism he had thought to give to the Fatherland at war to the peace effort instead, the hearts of these persecuted people went out to him. They came to be proud of him – and their pride had the same roots as their resentment of other members of the governing social class. Turncoats are invariably overrated. It was to this principle that Paul owed his importance in revolutionary circles.

It was interesting to observe that Paul's dissident attitudes did nothing to diminish the martial splendour of his appearance. He sparkled and clinked as he walked. He combined the charisma of the hero with the fervour of the rebel. Several badges in his cap, the braid on his tight-fitting tunic, a short sword instead of an officer's revolver in a creaking red leather sword-belt, soft yellow boots and an extravagantly wide pair of riding breeches: such was his appearance, that of a god in the commissariat. His service consisted of the purchasing and requisitioning of cattle and grain, and his orbit was the hinterland, the communication area around the base, and occupied enemy territory. He toured cities and provinces, and he dined and slept in the houses of landowners, whose love of their country was not sufficient to keep them from trying to charge Paul excessive prices for their produce, and from pleading to have their requisition quotas reduced. The blandishments of his victims had no effect on him. The state might have lost a hero, but it gained an incorruptible quartermaster. For Paul requisitioned and drove bargains with all the ardour of a revolutionary. Personal conviction supported him in his official duty, and the fear of his victims flattered him every bit as much as the esteem of his fellow-pacifists. His conscientiousness was valued by his superiors. It shielded him from any possible suspicion. Thus he succeeded in uniting military virtues with anti-military principles. Just as he had once been able to read highbrow books, conduct intelligent conversations, and then utter smooth platitudes in female company, so now he was able to chat in officers' casinos and country seats, to play operetta tunes on the piano and dance with gusto, and at the same time plan his next article, think about a forthcoming demonstration, and prepare a speech. Passion and beliefs are tangled in the hearts and minds of men, and there is no such thing as psychological consistency.

One day, a few miles south of Kiev, Paul came across the bailiff Nikita Bezborodko. Bezborodko claimed to belong to an ancient Cossack family. Strong, fearless, wily and bold, he had already held off several requisition orders, cheated army purchasers of sizeable sums, sabotaged commands, delivered the wrong goods, and instead of providing the army with the agreed number of healthy horses, sent them animals that were diseased or blind.

In Paul Bernheim he met with opposition for the first time. Paul brought charges against the Cossack, but somehow it never came to a hearing. Then Paul ran into him at the railway station in Shmerinka.

'Good day, lieutenant!' said the Cossack.

'Haven't you been put away?'

'As you see, lieutenant, I haven't! I have friends in high places.'

They drank a few glasses together. They were sitting in an improvised bar, a dark unfurnished wooden shack, through whose tiny, unglazed windows the birds flew and the wind whistled. Then the Cossack said:

'I've got some pamphlets you might recognise here, lieutenant!'

'I'm having you arrested,' replied Bernheim, and stood up. The Cossack stood by the door, with a broad smile on his face and a knife in his right hand.

'Put your hands up!' he cried, with laughter in his voice.

Bernheim couldn't tell whether the Ukrainian was a spy in the service of the military police, or a revolutionary, or if he'd got his hands on the pamphlets by chance, or even if he was drunk or not. Evening was drawing in, the wind howled, and Paul Bernheim determined to get hold of the pamphlets, whatever happened. He could always say later in his defence that he had meant it as a ruse.

With his left hand, the Cossack tossed him a bundle, but remained standing by the door, the drawn blade in his right. He seemed to grow taller in the dusk. A silvery glow emanated from his sand-coloured coat, his pale grey fur cap, his yellow rawhide boots, his grey eyes. His head grazed the roof of the shack. The taller he seemed to become, the more Bernheim felt himself shrinking. A panic, surfacing from long-forgotten childhood years, the memory of ghostly dreams, grisly imaginings in darkened rooms, clutched at the grown man with a thousand arms. The schnapps, which usually never affected him, today blurred his mind, because he hadn't eaten. 'Why did I come in here with him?' It was the only clear and complete sentence his brain was capable of forming. Otherwise, it was only half-sentences that flashed through it, and the expression 'final hour' kept recurring like a pain, gone for a moment, but always expected to return, and finally even welcomed, because the agony of waiting was worse.

Suddenly Bernheim thought of another phrase. A phrase so foolhardy it would not have affected his judgement at any other time. One of those empty phrases, fragments of conventional slogans, pedagogical formulae, prescribed works of literature or legends adapted for children, that nestle in our brains for a whole lifetime, remaining dormant like bats while we're awake, but only waiting for the first sign of our consciousness dimming to start circling in us again. Such a phrase now occurred to Bernheim, and it was: 'an ignominious death'. An infantile notion it may be, but it is still capable of inducing a wiser man to mobilise what is called his masculinity. And in Paul Bernheim there were still certain notions that as a pacifist he was unwilling to admit to – the notion of 'a worthy end' for instance – because, however short, a spell with the dragoons is never entirely without effect. No sooner had his dimming brain come up with the phrase than he did the most stupid thing it was possible to do in his position. He went for his revolver, like a hero. In a trice, Bezborodko's knife was embedded in his right arm. He saw the door of the shack fly open, and the last, greenish light of day illuminated the dark shack. Then the wooden door slammed shut – Paul Bernheim was still conscious of the sound – and it was dark once more. Bezborodko was gone.

Paul made no attempt to pull the knife out of his arm. The darkness of the room around him seemed to breed another, even blacker darkness inside him, which seemed to pour from his optic nerve into his eye, as the external darkness poured through his retina. Blackness, within and without. He didn't know whether his eyes were open or shut. The pain seemed to ring in his arm, as though the blood pulsing against the steel made a metallic chime.

He awoke some hours later with a bandaged arm, on a sofa in the room of the Jewish innkeeper, and fell asleep again immediately.

A few days later he left Shmerinka. The pamphlets had vanished. The whole episode seemed unreal to him, like a dream, and he almost began to wonder whether he had actually been wounded by Bezborodko. He too had vanished.

33

Nevertheless, the incident robbed him of the certainty in which he had been living. The war was already into its third year. Who can say whether it was fear or conscience that now caused Paul Bernheim to forsake his pleasant duties, and to volunteer for service at the front? It was as though Death, which had brushed past him in the shack, had left him a taste of its terrible black and red sweetness, and started a craving for it in Paul. He forgot about his friends and their journals and meetings. He deserted their camp, as he had previously deserted to enter it.

So manifold and unfathomable is a man.

4

And so Paul Bernheim went up to the front.

It was a cold, dreary day in November – the rain falling from the sky mingled with the mists rising from the earth – when Bernheim travelled unaccompanied to the battle-field.

He was now a lieutenant in the Xth infantry regiment, which for some weeks past had been occupying a position in the southern sector of the Eastern Front. 'You're in luck,' his new comrades on the staff had said to him. 'That's the quietest front there is right now. A few days ago, and you'd have had to go and find us in the Alps: that was Hell!' Paul would rather have joined his regiment in the Alps, where Death was more at home than in the east. It spoilt the resolve with which he'd joined the infantry, determined to make a change in his life, the fact that the Eastern Front was being called 'idyllic'. In his present condition he wanted the most powerful experiences, the gravest dangers, the worst assignments. It was, he told himself, a question of exploiting his rare and happy condition of resoluteness so thoroughly that it became permanent. He was afraid it might pass, without bringing the hoped-for gains. After all, it was only his old inconstancy, which had so far taken him the way of art history, England, the cavalry and pacifism. Just as he had once wanted to be the perfect Englishman, he now wanted to be the perfect infantryman.

But he himself had little insight into these secret motivations of his. Above them, dense and heavy as the November day, lay a dreary fog of indifference. He'd been sitting in the cold second-class compartment for hours now, alone. Another passenger who had shared it with him for a couple of hours had got out long ago. Although it wasn't yet evening, it was a grey afternoon, and the gas lamp spluttered, greasy and yellow, reminding Paul of the candles on the graves on All Souls' Day. From time to time he wiped his sleeve over the misted window to check that the train was actually moving. He saw the November rain falling like a grey curtain over this hinterland that was just starting to turn into the base area, and behind it were small valleys, scattered and abandoned farms, women with their skirts wrapped over their heads, the black shapes of kaftanned Jews, yellow stubble fields and twisting roads, whose black mud gleamed in the rain, telegraph poles, broken or upright, field-kitchens, lost and half-buried in the muck, marching supply troops, dark brown shacks, railway tracks and little stations, at every one of which his train stopped. It also stopped frequently between stations. It was as though the train itself had misgivings about the battle-field it was heading towards, and was using any opportunity to stop and wait for a ceasefire.

However absurd the thought was, and however bizarre Paul's apprehension that he might get to the war too late, the possibility did keep crossing his mind that they were just in the process of making peace out here, and that he would find himself in the atrocious position of returning to civilian life as he was, unchanged, and still stained with the memory of his late, humiliating encounter with the Cossack. His current requirements were for a war that would go on for at least another five years. That was how desperate he felt about peace, home, his mother, the bank, the servants and employees. When he remembered that not long ago he had written and delivered blazing protests against the war, these last months and years seemed incomprehensible to him. They had been bewilderingly eclipsed by that terrible, unfathomable experience with Nikita. A man had threatened him, defeated him, left him wounded, and disappeared. Nothing more. 'Yes, but this man perhaps knows everything about me, more than I know myself. He holds my life in his hands – he can destroy me – and I can't find him, he's disappeared forever. But my life' – he comforted himself – 'my life is in my own hands as long as I'm at the front. I can die at any moment. And if the Ukrainian does happen to know something, I'll deny it. I'll brazen it out, and they'll believe me. One or other of my former friends and comrades may have betrayed me. I'll deny it. They've got no proof. The articles aren't even in my hand, I had them typed under an assumed name. Who cares anyway?'

Whenever the train stopped, he would feel soothed by the monotonous melody of the rain, falling with soft tenacity over hundreds of miles, suspending the distances and distinctions between landscapes and places. The world was no longer one of mountains, valleys and villages, it was one of November. From time to time

37

Paul's worries would be submerged in this leaden indifference. He would identify with one or other of the defenceless objects on the field, exposed to the rain, with the smallest, most inconsequential, inanimate of things, a straw for instance, lying there passively, blissfully awaiting its end, insofar as it could be capable of feeling happiness. A stream might pick it up and sweep it away, a boot heel might crush it.

For the first time Paul had a sense of the war, and like the millions of enlisted men, he felt the lofty equanimity of those who threw themselves blindly onto the mercy of a blind fate. 'I'll probably die,' he thought, a sweet comfort. And as the evening wore on, and the black wall of darkness rose on the other side of the window, and the dim light grew stronger in the compartment, for long moments he felt like a dead man, a dead man in an illuminated mausoleum. Life's joys and anxieties, its hopes and fears, all lay far behind him. He had escaped them all. For a fugitive like himself, there was no more certain destination, no safer refuge, than the front and death.

He remembered the will he had drawn up before embarking on this journey. In the event of his death, almost everything was to go to his mother, and very little to his brother, whom his father hadn't mentioned in his will at all. Paul shooed away the thought of Theodor, he didn't want to think of him. Although he was going willingly, even gladly, to his death, there was always a violent little pang of envy of his younger brother, secure in his youth, secure from the war, secure in the expectation of seeing its end, and the better times afterwards. 'He doesn't deserve it!' Paul said to himself. He returned to the bliss of his own forebodings instead.

In his present mood, he exaggerated the length and the richness of the years he'd lived. Even this exaggeration was dictated to him by his arrogant self-belief. 'I was wealthy,' he told himself, 'young and strong and attractive. I have had women, known love, seen the world. I can die without regrets.' Suddenly the memory of Nikita struck him again. 'I should have gone to the front earlier,' he thought. 'I shouldn't have opposed the war. I'm not going willingly to my death now, I'm being chased. It serves me right.'

As the night went on, it became colder. Paul tried to turn out the lamp. He wanted to lie in the dark, so that his sense of being in the grave should be complete. He wanted to lie in a grave rolling to the next world. The lamp wasn't to be extinguished, though. It was the Light Everlasting that had been lit for the salvation of his soul. He was unable to sleep. With frozen fingers, he tried to write something in his notebook. Writing clears your mind, he thought. He was incapable of writing so much as a line, and instead he started doodling pointless decorations on the white page, as he had once done in his religion class. He remembered his classmates, and began to sketch some of their faces. He recreated the entire class, the benches, the teachers.

He spent the whole night occupied like this.

By morning the rain had turned into sparse hail and glassy snow that pattered softly against the windows.

The train was approaching the last station. This was the edge of the world. A horse-drawn, narrow-gauge railway began here, leading directly to regimental HQ.

Paul rode in the low open wagon with a few soldiers returning from leave. He heard their singing against the sound of the distant barrage, as through a thick wall. He barely felt the wind and the icy, stabbing rain. He saw the first of the wounded, hobbling back in their white bandages, on the arms of orderlies, trailing blood on the wet black earth and the thick, soft, yellow clay. He stood in the corner, hands in his pockets, collar turned up, watching them leave the front, the dazzling white, the vermilion blood, the encrusted grey of the uniforms, the black mud underfoot. The sound of gunfire became more distinct now, the soldiers stopped their singing, a second evening drew in.

He reached his regiment at nightfall, and had an unexpected piece of luck, as he thought at the time. An enemy attack was expected later that very night. All the men were writing field-postcards home. Not because he really wanted to, but so as not to attract attention, Paul wrote to his mother. 'Maybe she'll cry over me,' he said to himself, and he thought of his father's funeral, and the tears in the glittering ice-eyes of his mother. He had no message for his brother Theodor.

But then he didn't die! Not Paul Bernheim! A bayonet pierced his right cheek. He reached the field-hospital in the morning. They operated on his jaw. While his wound was healing, he contracted typhoid, and was packed off to an epidemic hospital behind the lines. It was as though old Felix Bernheim was watching over his son, probably still proud of him, from Heaven; as if the luck that had brought the old man lucrative deals and a jackpot now kept the young one from death. For it was only now, as

40

he lay in a fever with four others in the officers' section of the barracks, that the fear of death awakened in Paul, and the will to remain alive, when for the preceding days life had been a thing of such indifference to him. He believed fervently that he would survive, and took the lucky wound he'd sustained as fortune's promise to him that he would be spared. And even though every other day one of his comrades beside him would turn ghastly blue and rigid, even in the highest and most delirious fever, Bernheim knew at all times that he would not die.

His condition improved. He left that hospital, caught a cold, developed pneumonia, and went into another one.

This new illness seemed to be a further consequence of his will to stay alive and never to set foot on a field of battle again. He had long ago managed to push his encounter with Nikita to the back of his memory. He became the old Paul Bernheim again. He lay in his bed by the window, and felt that he had come out on top and proved himself cleverer than the rest of the world. His old arrogance came to his bedside like a good, trusty friend. A bluish nightlight shone over the door. The hurried, sawing, panic-stricken breathing of a sick comrade sounded inhuman in his ears, as though produced by some strange unfamiliar animal. In the blue light, which reminded him of the moon on a winter's night, Paul Bernheim saw the last obstacle he still had to overcome. He protested against the innocent lamp. That lamp kept a man like Paul Bernheim, whose requirements were naturally different from those of the common or garden invalids, from lighting a candle to read, or write, or sketch. Not only did one have to have the smell of carbolic and iodine in one's nostrils day and night, one wasn't permitted to read when one pleased either. The large, beautiful rooms at home! Paul Bernheim could remember the exact pattern of the wallpaper, the warm, golden chime of the breakfast gong, the Tchaikovsky duets he had played with his sister. There was a difference as great as the difference between sickness and health between the silence in the hospital, the acrid smell of the wards, the sacrificial white of the doctors' coats, the sighing and fatigue of his comrades, the wing-beat of death constantly overhead – and Paul's alert, eager and exalted longing for life. Paul Bernheim was proud of his recuperation, as if it had been all his own doing. He looked down on the sick as inferior beings. He had a low opinion of the doctors because he hated the stench of carbolic. He had got into the habit, whenever one of them came up to his bed, of seeing in him a mere dentist, only promoted to full medical practice for the duration of the war. For in Paul Bernheim's opinion a dentist was inferior to a surgeon, just as in that of his mother a civil servant was superior to a banker. In every nurse he would see a housemaid. This was his secret revenge on the hospital for its rules which didn't take sufficient account of his particular wishes. It was as if those few hours during which he'd decided he had finished with life, and hadn't been so taken up with his own person as he had been for the rest of it, now demanded to be paid for by a double quantity of arrogance. Perhaps Paul Bernheim's character would not permit even a brief period of modesty, and was determined to make up for it. For it is not the case that suffering, danger and nearness to death

42

inevitably change a man. They could do nothing to Paul Bernheim.

His convalescence took so long that he played no further part in the war. When he was discharged from hospital he got leave, and before that was over the Revolution had broken out.

In those days, it should be said, Paul Bernheim was not afraid to appear in the streets wearing the badges of his rank. In fact, he refused to wear civilian clothes. It was not out of respect for his uniform, because he belonged to a defeated army, and while he despised many things, he despised nothing so much as what had been defeated. On the contrary, he was pleased because now his pacifist phase would certainly not be held against him. With quiet pride, he reflected that it was England, *his* England, that had won. It was as though history had justified Bernheim's Anglomania, and, whenever there was talk of the war, his expression seemed to say: 'I knew it all along.' In spite of all that, he still refused to take off his insignia just to please some private. In his opinion a revolutionary Fatherland was no better than a defeated one.

And so it came about that one day he was beaten up by a few soldiers, and a few right-wing newspapers saw in him the personification of heroic, patriotic duty. It was the first time he had seen his real name in print. And, as though he'd never opposed the war, never preferred life to death on the field of battle, and never preferred England to his Fatherland, he began to think like a conservative and a patriot, and he could see himself becoming a member of parliament and a minister.

Yes, it had to be a minister.

5

Paul Bernheim would have liked to announce his return by telephone. However, telephoning Frau Bernheim was not altogether straightforward. She was incapable of understanding anything if she didn't have the speaker in her sight. At the very least, she had to be able to see him in her mind's eye. Not until she had a picture of him could she begin to understand. It was as though human speech was a very imperfect form of communication in Frau Bernheim's world, something with which to back up looks and gestures. Perhaps this was why her own use of words was so reckless and inappropriate.

So Paul telegraphed his return. But telegrams could also trouble Frau Bernheim. In her opinion the telegraph had been invented specifically for the speedy and reliable transmission of bad news. Gradually, since becoming a widow, and even more since the outbreak of the war, she had begun to 'tighten her belt' – as she loved to say – and whenever she received a telegram from Paul, she would calculate how much it had cost. Her joy at the news of Paul's return, on reading the telegram, was roughly equal to her fright on its arrival, and her regret at its expense. And it took rather a long time before she could comprehend the message in all its joyful import, disentangled from her fear and her compulsion to count up the words.

She had known about Paul's wound and his long illness, but since he had neglected to tell her of his transfer to the infantry, her implicit faith in the cavalry had seen her through. Even when she heard of his wound, it didn't occur to her that he might die of it. Being wounded in the cavalry was to her tantamount to cutting oneself with one's penknife. Typhoid held no dangers for mounted men. 'Paul is an officer,' she would say, 'and I'm sure they'll take good care of him.' Not for an hour of the war had she been concerned for her son's safety, but day and night about money. She was terrified that she might become poor. All the time, she saw, there was little income but plenty of outgoings. Herr Merwig, an old employee of her husband's, came to her every month and reported on the state of the business. The end of the war, the Revolution, the cripples on the streets, and the number of beggars who, in her words, were 'battering down the doors', so exercised her that the prospect of Paul's return brought her no more than a few minutes of happiness and excitement. That evening, when Theodor came home, she showed him the telegram. He folded it away neatly, put it down on the table without a word, and picked up the newspaper. Frau Bernheim snatched at the lorgnon that always dangled, weapon-like, at her hip, clicked it open, raised it to her eyes and gazed at her son, as though she were gazing at the stage. She was fond of using her lorgnon when she was cross. She had discovered that the servants were afraid of it. Theodor heard the click, and buried his face even deeper in the newspaper.

Frau Bernheim dropped the lorgnon again. After a moment she said: 'You've got no more heart than your father did. But at least he was clever. He had wonderful business sense. On top of everything else, you're bone idle. You've done nothing these last years. If it hadn't been for those marvellous retakes, you'd still be at school, or you'd have become a cobbler. You remind me more and more of dear cousin Arnold. He got into debt and died in an asylum. Even that cost money, otherwise he'd have had to go to prison.'

She waited a few minutes. Then, as Theodor was still reading the newspaper, she suddenly screamed: 'We've got no money, Theodor, d'you hear? We can't afford to save idlers from prison! You'll be put in a cell, d'you hear?!'

Theodor covered his ears with his hands, and went on reading the newspaper.

'Put that newspaper away when your mother's talking to you,' she added, a little quieter now.

Theodor immediately put his hands down, but didn't stop reading.

Sometimes he was able to remain silent for so long that she would sigh loudly and leave the room. Today, though, she would not give up. She began talking once more, unspooling slow, even sentences like thread, in a nagging monotone. Theodor thought each sentence would never end. Frau Bernheim emphasised the insistency of her speech by slowly and evenly smoothing the tablecloth. Deliberately, incessantly, to the rhythm of her voice, her palms ran along the edges of the table in either direction. Although Theodor was immersed in the newspaper, he had become aware of his mother's white, blue-veined hands, and little by little he became as terrified of these weak old woman's hands as if they had belonged to a murderer. He didn't budge. He stopped reading. The columns of newsprint blurred in his gaze. But he did not show it, and to prove that he was entirely set on his reading, he slowly turned the pages to the rhythm of his mother's speaking, entirely hypnotised by it.

'Any decent man would be pleased to have his brother come home from the war,' said Frau Bernheim. 'But you're sorry Paul didn't die. Don't think a mother doesn't know everything about her children, and God is my witness, and your dear departed father knows it as well, though he never believed me when I told him what a wicked child you were, evil as a spider and fickle as a cat and stupid as a donkey. There's a whole menagerie inside you, and all your upbringing was in vain, it just isn't possible to bring up children, as I always told Felix, if they haven't got it from birth, a soul is what it is, I suppose, and that's it, you haven't got a soul. If you weren't too frightened to, you would strike your old mother, you'd like to see me dead, wouldn't you, as a corpse. But I won't die away quietly until I know you've become a decent human being, but you're not capable, what do you do with yourself, going around all day with your friends, who I don't like the look of, when Paul was your age he would be out dancing, he was a wonderful dancer and swept beautiful young ladies right off their feet, and he didn't spend all day lying in the woods, shooting guns like you do, I'm afraid of your pistols and your knives too, Anna doesn't want to tidy up in your room any more, am I supposed to – '

A dark blush, almost blue, covered Theodor's face. He flung the newspaper to the floor. He got up, kicked the chair over behind him, his small, rolling eyes behind the black-rimmed spectacles seemed to be scouring the long, broad table for some object to throw at his mother. Finding nothing, he started shouting out wildly, like a chant:

'Pick up the newspaper, pick it up, pick it up mother, pick up the newspaper, mother, mother!'

In a trice, he had recovered his pallor.

His thin, flat, yellow face was like a loaf of bread that wouldn't rise. It was concave rather than convex. Right up to its very tip, which was delicate, blunt and bloodless, the nose seemed to be part of the cheeks. The lips were thin and didn't quite cover the long teeth. As with many people who carry their heads low between raised shoulders, his chin stuck out. His ears were yellow, large and translucent like parchment, and they had no rims, as though there hadn't been enough substance to provide any. Over the low forehead, which was furrowed like an old man's by four or five horizontal wrinkles and two thick vertical ones, there was the thin, light-blond hair, rigorously combed upwards. The watery eyes behind the glittering spectacles had a frightened expression, as though they had just seen a fire. The voice grew high and whining. One might have thought Theodor was crying for help from his mother, and not crying to her to pick up the newspaper. He started to tremble. To prevent his teeth from chattering, he clenched his jaws. His tongue pressed against his teeth, he was uttering almost unintelligible stammering cries:

'P-pick up the newsp-pepper, p-pick it up, p-pick it up!'

Frau Bernheim, who took a certain pleasure in these outbursts of Theodor's, picked up her lorgnon again. She enjoyed such moments. They were the only times when she could feel really superior – and when logic would suddenly rouse itself in her, as though stimulated by her son's complete irrationality. Although her mouth never moved, there was a glimmer of a smile in her hard eyes, as her voice quietly took advantage of a moment during which Theodor stood dumb and breathless:

'There was no need for you to fling the newspaper down on the floor. But even if there had been, your mother wouldn't have to pick it up for you. Bend down yourself, it'll do you good. Just as much good as prowling around in the woods. Bend down, boy, bend down!'

She spoke these sentences in a soft, motherly voice in which the malice was packed like a frail steel instrument in cotton wool.

Theodor left the room. Frau Bernheim stayed looking at the door a moment after he'd slammed it. She waited for the echo to fade.

Then she bent down, picked up the newspaper, and started reading it.

Theodor went into the hall.

He was smiling. He tried to tread softly. His shortsightedness made him cautious. He craned his neck, and looked this way and that. He approached the dresser opposite the cloakroom. On the second shelf on the left was the tin collecting-box. It had been given to Frau Bernheim once by a charity, which purposed coming to empty it once a month. But Frau Bernheim preferred to see for herself how her money was spent. Receipts were not sufficient. She used the tin to keep change for the beggars who came to her regularly on a certain day of the week.

There was a tiny lock dangling from the tin. Theodor had already tried to pick it a few times with the keys in his large collection. He knew that nothing would hurt Frau Bernheim more than if this money – the giving of which already caused her such heartache – were to be stolen.

First, he took the tin into his room. He locked the door, and tried out his little keys one after another, thought a while, picked up a knife, and cautiously prised at the gap between tin and lock. His heart pounded with terror and joy . . . For a moment he put the tin down, and tried to imagine his mother's reaction. 'The bitch!' he said to himself, aloud. He listened. Nothing stirred, and he turned the tin upside down. The rattle was louder than he had expected. He listened again. He opened the door to check there was no one outside. Then, with infinite care, he began the process of removing the coins, one by one. Some rolled smoothly and obediently through the crack. Others remained obdurately in the tin. He became tired and sat down. He had the persistence of a poacher. He worked far into the night. At last there were only a few coins left rattling about in the tin. Then he carefully squeezed the slit shut again, crept outside, and put the tin back in its place.

He counted the money. It was just enough for the monthly subscription to the 'God and Iron' society to which he'd belonged for the past two years.

50

The society had been founded by a young man by the name of Lehnhardt. With the exception of the founder himself, who was middle class, all the members were to be of noble origin. But after two months, there were only four of these. Accordingly, the statutes were changed, to the effect that only 'fair-haired men of Aryan families' were acceptable. On closer inspection, however, it transpired that the founder's own hair was really more brown than fair. Still, they turned down the son of a local judge, who had black hair. He went to his father and complained that Lehnhardt and Theodor Bernheim had called him a Jew. Very irate, the judge summoned the two boys to him, and persuaded them to accept his son. So, in its final form, the statute merely excluded Jews from the society.

They lent one another books, money and weapons. They swore that, having successfully retaken their exams, they would always remain in contact. For the moment, they reported to the voluntary ambulance service. They had 'duty spells', went to the wounded transports, carried stretchers, sat next to the ambulance drivers and blew their shrill whistles in the streets of the town to clear them of other traffic. Every day they got up, hoping to hear that their year had been called up. When peace finally came, they swore to avenge themselves on the Republic, established contact with secret groups and went marching off to exercise twice a week outside town.

Theodor did not shine at these exercises. He was ill-suited to physical exertion. The pallor of his skin, his short, hasty steps, his voice that easily lost its timbre, the excitement with which he said rather routine things, the

51

jerkiness of his movements, all gave one the impression of hearing his fluttery pulse. He seemed to have a bird's heart in his chest, small, wriggling and excited. He would walk up to someone with an expression of just having heard surprising news, and then utter some banality like: 'Have you heard? Did I tell you? I got a letter yesterday from Gustav.'

The most trivial events had an allure of significance, danger and secrecy for him, especially secrecy. He delighted in knowing something before the others did; but also in passing it on to one of them, under pledge of secrecy. It was his precarious way of bolstering his belief in his own importance.

He was very taken with public life and big words like Honour, Freedom, Nation and Germany. He was desperate to make his mark in some way. His fear of falling ill with angina or bronchitis or pneumonia or pleurisy spurred him on. He could barely ever finish a book. It only took him ten pages to become wildly enthusiastic about it, or to adjudge it 'putrid'. He was given to forceful expressions. It was perhaps the only clear indication of his youthfulness.

He thought of himself as rather refined. Occasionally he would dream of writing a family history, of tracing the Bernheim family tree and finding evidence that they were indeed an ancient noble line. His mother's Jewish ancestry worried him. Not even illness frightened him as much as the possibility of having to tell his comrades the truth about his mother's family. He resolved to lie at all costs. This resolve was so strong – his fear was so strong – that it gradually turned into the conviction that he actually had nothing to hide. In time, he came to believe that all his distortions and inventions were true.

His conviction of his own refinement manifested itself in his conceit, which his comrades only put up with because he would occasionally vary it with confidences, intimacies, even flattery. Theodor was capable of telling one of his comrades: 'Between you and me, you're the only one of them who knows what he's after!' Or: 'That was wonderful, that was a real achievement!'

One must assume Theodor believed such things at the time he was saying them.

He was an unwilling participant in group excursions and training. Not only because he was concerned for his health, but also because coarse expressions, importunities and tasteless remarks offended him. He had come to believe so strongly in his refinement that his sensibilities had actually become finer. Marching, shooting and camping in the open were no fun for him. It was only the fact that here was a secret association, offering danger and the chance to be a conspirator – and also the attention of the like-minded – that kept him in the society of his friends. He had no love for jackboots and puttees. The *Wandervogel*'s closeness to nature was vulgar to him. 'For the future' – one of his favourite phrases – he looked rather to science. He had a sincere desire to see the German people triumphant in the world, but by modern methods. By aeroplanes, boxers, good cheap automobiles, chemical processes, astonishing machines. Secretly, he thought of exercises in the woods as merely romantic. Only for the time being he was required to participate in this form of romanticism in order to gain

53

real power, or at any rate real influence. Having to lie first mattered little him. That was one of his principles.

He couldn't get to sleep that night. It wasn't just that his mother would worry herself to death over the empty tin – yes, to death – because if she wasn't there, that would be one thing less for him to be afraid of: its contents also saved him the pocket money he only rarely received.

His joy was only dimmed by the thought of Paul's return.

'I can see,' he said to himself at two in the morning, 'I'm going to have another sleepless night. And it's gone and started raining too.'

Indeed, there was a whispering in the gutter that ran down beside Theodor's window. He lit the lamp on his beside table, found its light insufficient, got up to switch on the main light in the room, first putting on his spectacles because he felt unsafe in the half-light, and then stopped in front of the wardrobe mirror on his way back to bed. He was pleased to see that his pyjamas made a good impression. They shimmered like silk, the borders were as thickly braided as a cavalry tunic, and their colour had the opalescence of a summer evening. Theodor loved pyjamas, fine linen, silk socks. It was a mark of refinement for him, to be immaculately dressed at night. To tie his cravat swiftly and neatly delighted him every morning. And one of the arguments that had swayed him to accept the judge's son into the society was that he subscribed to gentlemen's fashion magazines, which he would occasionally lend to Theodor.

In order to sleep, Theodor would take Veronal. There

was a chance it might be 'bad for his heart'. One of his fears was that the apothecary might make a mistake and give him poison instead of medicine. Stupid druggists, he thought, poisoning a man like a rat. If one of those apothecaries should take a dislike to you, he'd simply do away with you, just like that. Best be polite to the fellows. I'll be nice to him tomorrow. He referred to all men as 'fellows'. There were two kinds of fellow: those he envied and those he despised.

His brother Paul was one of those fellows he both envied and despised. 'So the fellow's turning up here tomorrow! He's young, healthy and rich, a typical stingy Sunday child. Will he give me a penny of it? Not a chance. A miser.' (For it was one of Theodor's peculiarities to think of both the envied and the despised 'fellows' as misers.) 'He's coming tomorrow to take possession of the whole house. He and mother will join forces against me. I'll greet him haughtily. The way I can.'

'The way I can,' he repeated in a whisper. Fear had gripped him again. The Veronal didn't help, it caused palpitations, the gutter carried on whimpering, gusts of wind blew drops of water as big as pebbles against the windows. Theodor started leafing through a book he'd found in Paul's library. It was called *The Rembrandt-German*. He came upon a sentence that pleased him, and decided to memorise it and quote it to Lehnhardt when he spoke to him the next day. The effort made him sleepy.

Pale morning filled the window.

6

Theodor woke late.

He heard Paul's voice in the corridor, and decided he would stay in bed for another couple of hours, to put off his reunion with his brother for as long as possible. His mother knocked on the door. He gave no reply beyond a little cough. He heard her go away again, and say something to Paul in the dining room.

He dressed with special care, and pinned his 'God and Iron' badge on his lapel. He felt as though he were preparing for an encounter with a dangerous foe, and his instinct told him to be on his guard. It even pressed one of his three pistols into his hand as a final measure. Then, as though carrying out an ambush, he tiptoed up to the door of the dining room, listened a while, and went in.

The brothers embraced one another perfunctorily, and each kissed the air over the other's shoulder.

'What's that badge you're wearing?' asked Paul.

'That's our society!' replied Theodor.

'What do you get up to?'

'All sorts of things!'

Long pause.

Theodor, who couldn't endure silence, started walking up and down the room with his short strides, head lowered, right thumb hooked into the left breast of his waistcoat. One might have thought he was learning something by heart, or trying to solve a puzzle his brother had set him.

'You got up late today.'

'Yes!' grunted Theodor.

'You went to bed late last night?'

Theodor pricked up his ears. Did his brother know about the tin?

'Oh, you know how I can't sleep when it's raining, and anyway I was working late.'

'Studying?'

'Yes, I've been busy with Marx these last few months.' Theodor had a love of breathtaking lies. The astonishment of his interlocutor would be such that the result was often admiration rather than disbelief.

'Why Marx?'

'The fellow had ideas. He had instinct. And anyway, you should get to know your enemy before fighting him.'

'Are you thinking of writing a polemic against him?'

'Writing?! It's too late for that. I leave that to you. Our new race believes in deeds!'

'What are deeds?'

'What you do with mind and muscle. For instance: restore order in Germany, topple the government, ban the Bolsheviks and the Jews, light fires of celebration and declare war!'

'Are you speaking on behalf of your society?' asked Paul.

'I always do,' replied Theodor. 'We don't stand for individualists like you. We won't lose the next war.'

'Are you blaming me for the defeat?'

'Yes, you and the other Jews!'

'So it's war between us?'

'Enmity, at any rate. War if need be!'

'In that case,' Paul began after a while, slowly and calmly, 'we cannot live under the same roof. Perhaps we should ask mother – because by the terms of father's will, the house is hers – which of us should remain living here.'

'What do I care about legality. By your Judaeo-Roman principles, I'd probably be the one to have to go.'

'There is no Germanic law.'

'We'll see about that.'

Theodor went back to walking up and down, his thumb tucked into his waistcoat. He was trying to establish a position of calm and objective opposition.

'Have you ever read Marx?'

'No,' said Paul, 'only some rather inadequate things about him.'

Theodor thought an acknowledgement of certain Marxian principles would make his brother more conciliatory.

'Terrific stuff, Marx!'

Nothing could have infuriated Paul more than the phrase 'terrific stuff', and his brother's way of using it. Suddenly Theodor's presence seemed to hurt his eyes and weaken his hands, which he had to put in his pockets to conceal the fact that they were shaking.

'You're an imbecile!' said Paul suddenly. 'There are some elementary things you haven't begun to understand!'

'You're not competent to say that. Who are you?'

Theodor's voice grew louder. 'You and your "elementary things". That's all you know! You lost us the war with your "elementary things". We're embarking on a new era of German history. Your "elementary things" are rubbish! We're starting again. You don't have to have read Herder and Lessing to be a human being, or a German! It's only your wretched envy that makes you talk like that to us. You don't want to see us take over. You hate us! You're jealous because the future belongs to us! You and your classical education! It's the truth! You're a fool!'

The last sentence was so loud that Frau Bernheim came out of the kitchen. Before speaking, she brushed the back of her hand across her brow to squeeze from her obdurately dry eyes the tears she intended to use shortly. She stood in the doorway and said:

'Well, Paul, isn't your brother a silly boy?'

Theodor looked at his mother and brother as one might look at the dead bodies of one's enemies. He took out his handkerchief and started wiping his glasses. With his naked little eyes and eyelids flickering up and down, he looked at them alternately, thinking: They won't get away with it! Then he put his glasses back on.

Paul suddenly got up. He shook his fists in Theodor's face. Theodor reached for the revolver in his pocket. For an instant the scene with Nikita flashed through Paul's mind. He quickly went for Theodor's eyes. There was a quiet splintering of glass. The spectacles broke. Frau Bernheim screamed.

For a few moments all three stood motionless. They were like waxwork figures. The clock ticked from its bracket. The rain drummed against the window. One could hear the pipes gurgling in the corridor.

Then the group broke up. Frau Bernheim disappeared through the door. A little later Paul left the room and went into the library.

Theodor picked up the shards of glass, though he felt strongly inclined to let them lie. He didn't know yet what he was going to do with them. Put them in the cooking and kill everyone. Fling them across the table into Paul's eyes at lunch. Drop them in the salt. He cupped them in his hand. Head thrust forward blindly, he shuffled into his room. He put on a coat and changed his shoes for boots. He thought: I'm not about to do them the favour of catching pneumonia. And he left the house. He went first to the optician, and then to the 'God and Iron' society.

In the library, Paul saw that most of his books were missing. He went into Theodor's room, took a few off the shelves there and carried them back to the library. Then he returned to his brother's room. He studied the three brown shirts hanging from hooks with their sleeves dangling and swastikas sewn in black on a white ground. A walking stick was propped in a corner; there was a wire life-preserver concealed in the hollow cane. In addition, there was a hunting rifle, a pair of pistols in the drawer of the bedside table, and two daggers used as letter-openers on the writing-desk. The little cardboard boxes by the inkwell were full of bullets. There was enough here to keep a whole company at bay.

It was hot in the room, which as well as a central-heating unit contained a small iron stove. It wasn't lit now, but one could tell it had been burning all night. The stove gave the room something of the provisional character of a junior officers' messroom. Theodor used an umbrella frame for a poker. Near the stove hung two crossed rapiers and a fencing mask, a kind of shrine.

Theodor's was the only warm room in the house. Since Frau Bernheim had started economising, the porter was only allowed to turn on the heat when the temperature outside was down to 5° Centigrade. A savage chill clung to the furniture, the rugs and the windows in all the rooms. They resembled the cold, clear, tidy and eerily clean rooms in the windows of furniture shops. Everything was pristine and unused. The polish gleamed like new. The carpets seemed never to have picked up any dust. Several of them had been taken up by Frau Bernheim and stood in the corners of the rooms. They rested there, weighty and confident, as though they expected to be collected by someone. In the places where they had been, the flooring was linoleum, soft and smooth and brick-red – like indiarubber underfoot. Of the many clocks that Herr Felix Bernheim had had put into his redecorated house – when he was alive there had been one in every room, because of his weakness for them, and his knowledge that time was precious – only the one on the mantel in the dining room was still kept going. Frau Bernheim feared that their delicate mechanisms would run down with constant use. She left the dead clocks in their places, one in every room. From their meaningless white and silver faces, and the hands showing the same frozen hour for years, there radiated an eerie silence that stalked the frosty emptiness of the rooms.

Paul went through the house a couple of times. He stopped in front of his large portrait of his father. It was hanging in his father's study, over the bookcase whose top shelf had formerly housed odd books, newspapers and correspondence, but which today held only a solitary letter-balance with a gleaming brass pan that trembled very slightly, as if from the cold. The portrait of his father seemed to be looking at the balance. It had no other function left than to indicate the weightlessness of his dead expression. Paul looked for the real face behind the rather botched portrait. He couldn't find it. He remembered certain gestures of his father's body and his hands, their blue veins and square nails kept scrupulously clean, and almost white in colour. But the face was lost, it had never lived. Nor could opening the grave help. His father's face was now a thousand holes, and worms fed and lodged in it.

For the first time he felt sadness over his father's death. His father had been the only one in the family with any warmth or strength. Paul decided to leave. As long as his mother remained alive, no change could be expected. She would never let Theodor go. Paul would go himself.

He went into the garden. The straw-packed rose trees trembled, the young willow shrubs by the fence had grown somewhat, the gnomes dripped pathetically in the rain. Over the years they had lost their cheery colours, and the mossy green of decay had mingled with the snow-white of their fairytale beards. They had come as young and frisky sages, now they had lost the perky venerableness of their age, and were facing decay. Unlike men, the gnomes of Grützer & Co. were white-haired in their youth, and colourless in their old age. No gravel had been strewn on the paths, which no longer crunched underfoot. The little pebbles had all been swallowed up by the mud. On this cold, wet autumn day, the garden was more like a building site.

'Whatever happened to the gardener?' Paul asked his mother at the table.

'I dismissed him,' said Frau Bernheim. 'Or rather, he went into the army, and came home last week, but I didn't take him back. The porter manages quite well. We have to tighten our belts, Paul! I've sold the carriage and two of the horses, and rented some of the stalls out to Gerstner.'

'Who's he?'

'You remember, the dairy farmer. Since last year we haven't had a cook either, just the chambermaid. I've been doing the cooking.'

'It seems you've given up heating too.'

'There's coal in the cellar, only it won't last the winter if we start burning it now. What are we meant to do in January? And these times! The beggars are pushing down the doors, and they've become so impertinent. One of these days they'll ransack the house. There's no law nowadays! Merwig advised me to buy bonds. But what will I do with bonds, if something goes wrong?'

'But money's losing its value, mother!'

'Losing its value? Money?' cried Frau Bernheim. 'What else is going to be worth anything then?' It was as if she'd been told that the sun had risen for the last time that morning.

'It's better to buy shares,' Paul went on.

63

'For goodness' sake, Paul!' said his mother. 'What would a woman do with shares? What does a woman know about the stock exchange?'

'Leave it to Herr Merwig!'

'No, I can't do that. He urged me to buy war bonds. You should go round to the office and see him. I haven't liked him these last few months. Things are bad for him at home. His son's had both legs amputated, and has lost his job. Oh, these people! Employees are only honest as long as things are going well.'

She said it with her old 'majesty', the tone she still felt happiest in. Paul was offended by it, even though he'd never felt particularly warmly towards 'the staff'. 'But mother – Herr Merwig has been with us for thirty years!'

'Yes, and in the thirty-first he starts thieving,' said Frau Bernheim, and her lips clamped shut so tight that the skin tautened across her jaws and her face resembled a white stone.

Paul went along to Herr Merwig that very evening at the end of office hours. He found him sitting, as always, behind his partition of frosted glass, at his high desk. His thick grey moustache bristled, his stern eyes were the green of broken glass, his voice was a quiet grumble. He was a faithful servant, who no longer saw the difference between decency and meanness, and who had the absolute honesty of a rock.

'Things are going badly, Herr Paul,' said Merwig – and it sounded like a reproach, though it was only intended as a complaint. 'Since the master passed away, we've lost many clients. Most have gone to the big banks, all the smaller ones are in difficulties. They take up all sorts of shady business – not the kind of thing your late lamented father would have done at all.'

'Just refer to him as my late father, Herr Merwig,' Paul broke in. And so as not to have to listen to the old man any longer: 'We will make a fresh start, Herr Merwig. I will take personal charge.'

'It's time, Herr Paul –'

'Mother,' said Paul that evening, 'I will vouch for Herr Merwig. I have been over everything. He's only a little stupid.'

'The staff are always stupid, child. Did you happen to buy a newspaper? Theodor hasn't come home yet. Usually he brings one.'

'But don't we subscribe to it?'

'Not any more, child. I cancelled the subscription.'

'Why don't you send out for a newspaper then?'

'I thought you'd be bringing one, and Theodor, and then we'd have had three.'

'I'll go and get one.'

When Paul came home, there was a telegram on the table. 'Robert coming Wednesday. Kisses. Lina.'

There was Robert too. Paul had quite forgotten about him. What would they do with the cavalry captain?

'He'll have to be taken into the business as well,' said Frau Bernheim.

'But he doesn't know the first thing about it.'

'Never mind, I'm sure he'll pick it up as he goes along. A man of his stamp!'

Frau Bernheim had gone on judging men by their physical attributes. She loved her son-in-law. 'He's a fine figure of a man – you can tell he's a cavalryman even in his civilian clothes.' Paul reflected, with some bitterness, on how he himself had had to leave the cavalry. The cavalry was to blame for his encounter with Nikita, and his long illness. He didn't argue against Robert. When his brother-in-law arrived, he was even friendly to him. He was a nice, harmless man, really. Only he looked frightful in his civilian suit. His tie was far too thick, his hat dark green and far too small for him. Paul decided he would take Robert to a tailor, a hat shop, and a good barber.

He installed the now worldly-looking captain in the bank. In the end, he was quite pleased to have his brother-in-law there. A reliable man.

Paul took charge of so-called 'external business'. This he took to mean travelling. He rented an apartment in Berlin, and only came in to the bank once a week.

7

One afternoon, as Paul was just leaving his apartment, the porter said to him: 'Good morning, Herr Bernheim. You might care to know that the room directly above you on the second floor has become vacant.'

Paul had just got up. It was one of his characteristics to be especially interested by anything he discovered directly after getting up. He thus came to depend on the porter. Although the latter would receive foreign currency tips from Bernheim three times a week, he was still able to keep Paul continually feeling obliged to him, and perceiving a considerable discrepancy between the services the porter performed for him and the size of the rewards he received for them. To ignore the porter's hint would have been embarrassing to Paul. Moreover, it bothered him to know that there was an empty room directly overhead, which might be occupied by some still unknown, and therefore horrible, noise, such as a gaming club, for instance. And finally, he absolutely could not allow himself to be identified in the porter's mind as one of those tenants who fussed over a few valueless banknotes. So, as became a man of business, Paul enquired as to the rent. 'Ten dollars a month!' said the porter, who would not have dreamed of mentioning any other currency in Paul's hearing. 'I'll take it,' said Paul, with the same quickness and decisiveness with which he said on the telephone: 'Done, I'll buy!'

He could use another room. The further he walked down the Kurfürstendamm, the more essential the room seemed to be. It was a foggy day in February, and the grey beggars and cripples on the street corners seemed to be made of fog themselves. Visibility was about three yards, and the streetlights burned like desperate stars. Paul knew that he would have regretted not taking the room. It gave a little fillip to the day. He had received no mail. On days when his letter-box was empty, he felt doubly abandoned. Such days turned him to pessimism and superstition. He imagined there was some hostile power that kept his correspondents from writing to him, or imprisoned their letters at the post office, or caused them to disintegrate in the mailbags in the postman's van. He didn't use the regular mails himself. He sent telegrams or registered letters. So, all day yesterday and the day before, no one gave me a thought, Paul would say to himself when his letter-box was empty. I have many friends, but I am all alone. Not even Marga has written to me.

On such days, he would slowly and pleasurably anticipate the business correspondence that awaited him in his office in the centre of town. ('Downtown', he would say.) Otherwise, this correspondence had no interest for him whatsoever. A business friend had lent him an office, in which Bernheim's personal secretary and a typist would receive and note down telephone calls, conclude small 'transactions' themselves, and telephone Paul at home for instructions on larger ones. Every afternoon, an hour after getting up, Paul would go to this office. If he had received mail at home, he would take the car. On the days of no mail, he would walk, to taste his desolation to the full. But also to reach the point where the pain of abandonment turned into an agreeable melancholy, and to prolong the hope of some surprising bit of business correspondence. It was even possible some private letter might have been misdirected to the business address.

He now decided to give up his 'downtown' office, and move it into the room on the second floor over his flat. There were hours in the early evening that he had to spend alone in his room, when no friend called, no letter arrived, and the telephone didn't ring. Then he felt his solitude around him like a prison. The women he was involved with only occupied him when they were actually present. His regular girlfriend Marga lived in Vienna, and visited him once a month. She was a young actress who couldn't be expected to leave her theatre. He hadn't been able to find work for her on the Berlin stage. But even if he'd had Marga with him, his sense of desertion wouldn't have been any less. She needed him only because that was what convention demanded. He didn't love her either, but only followed the custom of keeping a mistress. It was good for his credit socially, and economically too.

It was difficult to be alone. Just as railway trains came from afar, so troubling thoughts came from solitude. When he was alone, he thought about Nikita, the hospital, England, his interrupted studies at Oxford. He was almost thirty now. To him the thirtieth year marked the last stage on the road to greatness. If one hadn't become an important figure by then, it was too late. Then the whole of life lost its point. Because for Paul to lead a mediocre life would be a betrayal of himself, his talents, his youthful promise and his dead father. When he imagined his future, he could only picture greatness or death. And the more glowingly he imagined greatness, the more death frightened him. There were times when its emptiness surrounded and even filled him.

To escape it, he surrounded himself with friends. They were people who sponged off him, shadows that had emerged from the fog of the time, and were formed from it. All of them moved in the vague, indefinite and constantly shifting terrain between art and gambling. They were connected with the theatre, with fine art, with literature, but they didn't write, didn't paint and didn't act. One started a magazine that lasted for a week. Another took an advance for a newspaper article he would never write. A third set up a theatre company for young performers, and was arrested after the opening night. A fourth let out his rooms to a gaming club, could no longer stay at home, and gambled away the rent he was paid in other gaming clubs. A fifth, who had studied medicine, performed abortions, but in the interests of discretion only in the circle of his friends, from whom he could earn no fees. A sixth organised spiritualist meetings, and was denounced by one of his own mediums. A seventh spied simultaneously for the state police and for foreign embassies, cheated them all and was afraid of retribution from them all. An eighth fitted up Russian emigrants with false passports and genuine residence permits. A ninth passed false information from secret nationalist organisations to the radical newspapers, which a tenth bought, before it could be printed, and was rewarded for doing so by moneyed conservatives. Those were the days in which it was demonstrated that in this world morality depends on the stability of the currency. An ancient truth, which had merely come to be forgotten over the long years in which money, incontestably, had had value. A society's values are determined by the index of its stock exchange.

Any of these people might call in at Bernheim's apartment any time of the night or day. He earned real money – foreign money – was the only one of them to do so, and was therefore superior to them. The more this superiority cost him, the more precious it was to him. On occasion, he liked to overestimate his friends in order to impress himself. He gave in to the illusion that he was leading the life of a true gentleman. As his father had done in his time, he now bought his suits, his shoes and his hats from England. He smoked English tobacco in English pipes, ate fruit and oatmeal and raw meat, and went riding, as he had done in his younger days. He regretted not owning a horse. He had an automobile on hire purchase, and a liveried chauffeur. Paul would have liked to own cars and a string of horses. Convinced like all the world that the politics of the national and international scene were governed by economics, he had forsaken his art-historical and literary interests, and spoke only of 'economic realities'. To Dr König, one of his friends, he would say: 'It's all about dominating the market. The market is public opinion. The newspapers are in hock to the banks. Whoever dominates the banks and their hirelings rules the state.'

Dr König, a man of the left who had Russian sympathies and thought of himself as a revolutionary without a revolution, listened with the respect that opponents of bourgeois society always have for that society's pillars. Bernheim thought of him as a mighty leader of the workers, while he saw Bernheim as the secret confidant of heavy industry. So they sat opposite one another, the representatives of hostile forces, seemingly as candid as old friends, and each consumed with the thought of the effect he was having on the other.

'In time we'll do business with Russia!' said Paul, with conciliatory irony.

'To earn back there what we'll have taken off you here,' replied Dr König.

In the evening they would sit side by side at the gaming tables. Dr König lost. He would attribute his ill-fortune to his political philosophy, which taught him to despise money. So he would borrow from Paul, who won, and explained it in the traditional way, by his misfortune in love. He had no stomach for politics in the evening. Rather the gossip of Kastner, who sometimes brought along works of pornography to flick through. Kastner got them as commission from people who were in financial difficulties. Bernheim had already purchased several such items from him. He used them to divert the ladies who visited him, first telling them: 'I must leave you for half an hour now, I have some business to attend to. Why don't you look at these magazines here. But be careful not to look at those works over there. They're poison for women!' When he returned, fifteen minutes later, he would find the woman poring over one of the banned books.

Several times a week he would give dinner parties that would go on until dawn. His chauffeur would play butler in a pair of white gloves. After dinner, a young writer would read aloud from his new play. The chandelier would be extinguished, and only the lamps in the corners left on, with dark batik shades over them.

The playwright would read from an armchair. The audience would recline on cushions, of which Bernheim owned about a hundred. They served as sofas. The more complicated the dramatic action became, the more the attention of the audience would stray to their female neighbours. By the time the writer got to the last act, most would be lying in darkness. For them the curtain had already fallen.

The batik lamps had gone out. Here and there a phantom hand reached out for a glass. In the next room, the chauffeur was playing soft music on the gramophone. Someone hummed along to it. A couple struggled to their feet, danced a few steps, and then fell back as though their clockwork had run down. Most had the strength to smoke a cigarette, and no more. Together with the smoke, they exhaled the sour taste in their mouths, and the compounded smell of wine, cigarettes, powder and scent somehow resembled that of menthol and tooth-paste. Before it grew light, the chauffeur, whose gloves by a miracle were still virginal white, glowing in the dark, brought round coffee in tiny cups. The ladies, and those of the gentlemen who wore gold bracelets, crooked their little fingers as they drank.

The guests left, one after another, without saying goodbye, on the cusp of night and day, as though the day frightened them. A full half hour after the last of them had gone, Paul still wouldn't know if he was alone again or not. Like a nightwatchman, he did the rounds of his rooms. In the first pallor of morning, he searched among the scattered and heaped-up cushions for sleepers. He would have liked to come upon a guest at this time. Only he was afraid to say so, lest they all stayed. When he had convinced himself that his rooms were once more deserted, he started to play some of the melodies of his youth. The leaden winter day crept up to the windows. Paul let his fingers wander over the keyboard, following their own memories. The sounds they produced took a while to reach his ears. It was like hearing a stranger playing in a distant room. The melodies coincided with the first sounds of the awakening streets. Paul remembered mornings in childhood, the brief eternity of the quarter hour between waking and getting up in which his doubly acute senses picked up the sounds of morning in distant streets and nearby rooms. The smell of freshly roasted coffee and of audibly frying eggs wafted through the house and out into the street. When Paul left the house, the smell accompanied him part of the way. The first of the farmers' wagons were rolling into town. Groaning heavily, as though made of iron ore, the district's watering-cart appeared on the corner. In those days it was still pulled by a pair of enormous carthorses who seemed to be counting their own thunderous hoofbeats. The singsong cries of the street vendors echoed back from the walls of the empty courtyard, and from an open window came in reply the singing of a maid as she worked. One after another, Paul saw his classmates. He could still list them all alphabetically, as far as Morgenstern, then their names became submerged in the night of the past.

They've all gone on and become something, thought Paul, the ones that didn't die in the war. And how far behind me they used to be! With the unappeasable sobriety that follows a sleepless night, Paul unmasked his illusions one after another. These were the only hours in which he admitted the truth about his miserable set of friends and the false sheen of his affluence. It was as though the cheerful genuineness of the impressions echoing back from that distant time revealed the emptiness of the present, the way false pearls are shown up by real ones. His thirtieth birthday loomed like a menacing iceberg. Ambition tormented him like an incurable physical ailment. If only it would go away, thought Paul, if only it could be operated on. It wasn't part of his character, it was a redundant, diseased organ. As a miser counts up his unproductive treasures, so Paul counted up his unproductive talents. He could paint, play music, write, be entertaining, he knew something of business, of human beings, of economics, of world affairs. He wasn't doing badly, he was making money. But not enough to be powerful, and too much to know the consolatory bitterness of poverty. There had to be another secret, the secret of success. In time he might come upon it. A happy marriage perhaps.

Another day poured through the window, another terrible day. It brought with it emptiness, coldness and insight into the arid condition of things, an insight that gave rise to terror and roused the spectre of death —

salvation from mediocrity perhaps, but at what a price! And as a man closes his eyes before an imminent catastrophe, so Bernheim closed his eyes before the breaking day, and went to bed.

Work took up two hours a day at most. The business ran itself. A couple of telephone calls to Merwig at home brought him enough to live on for a month. He played on the difference between the dollar rates on the official and black markets of three cities. He had finally managed to persuade Merwig to get in touch with the black market people. Otherwise he'd have fired him. Without mercy, or in Paul's words, 'without weakness'. 'Don't start getting sentimental!' Paul would tell himself several times a day.

Now, with his office moved into the room above, he felt less lonely. There were people up there in his pay. They lived off him, so they had to be at his disposal. Unlike his friends, who thought their friendship reimbursed him for the money they borrowed. At about three in the afternoon he would slowly climb the stairs to his office. As he turned the key in the lock, a pair of typewriters would start rattling inside. Bent over them, as though they hadn't heard him coming, were the two girls. In the manner of female office personnel, they would hurl themselves like birds of prey over some insignificant letter, and grind it out between the rollers of their machines. An agreeable procedure to an employer, less on account of the industry evinced than because he enjoys striking fear in the hearts of his employees. Paul Bernheim too enjoyed such submissiveness. In accordance with the customs of the time, which was an epoch of swift and daring decisions, and in which, under the impact of the war, trade became like strategy, to the extent that deals had begun to be referred to as 'operations', Bernheim's eyes quickly surveyed the desks, and the correspondence which had been opened and laid ready for him. He liked it when he saw out of the corner of his eye his tremulously waiting secretary, not daring to disturb his master as he read. Paul Bernheim would then wax affable, another privilege of power.

'Well, go on then, show me what you've got!'

He studied the poor stuff his secretary's suit was made of, stiff and shiny, and felt the joy of boyhood, when with his term's report in his hand he said goodbye to classmates dreading a retake.

'Telephone deals?'

'Four so far,' said the secretary, 'General Realty, Farming, Credit and Mr Robinson.'

'Robinson? How many there?'

'Five hundred all told.'

'Chinese?'

'No, American.'

'Any news of Ergo Import Export?'

'The machines are selling poorly. If I might venture an opinion, there's little point.'

'No!' said Bernheim. 'No opinion,' – and in the soul of his secretary he read the words: 'He's right, who else pays fifteen dollars a week nowadays?'

'I think we'll keep an eye on it,' continued Bernheim. 'You have to have a feel for these things!' The telephone shrilled, and both the industrious girls stopped rattling right away. The secretary leaped to the receiver ahead of

Bernheim's outstretched hand. There was a momentary silence. It came from the two machines that had just been so noisy, and from the girls, who had a vacuous piety on their faces, the same expression with which they sometimes went to mass, or the weddings of strangers.

'Who is it?' Bernheim asked his secretary. He put down the mouthpiece with the conscientiousness and decision with which, for fifteen dollars a week, he would have put down every single telephone subscriber. Torn between the need to speak quietly and the fear that whispering might be disrespectful, he devised a pattern of broken telegraphese, as if to be ungrammatical was to remain discreet.

'Granich Düsseldorf asks, sign tomorrow!' he stammered.

'Have them wait!' Bernheim ordered, 'I'm in a meeting.'

The secretary spoke into the mouthpiece:

'So sorry, could you please wait or call back in an hour. Herr Bernheim is in an important meeting.' He thought it necessary to call the meeting 'important'. It would help to make him indispensable.

Paul Bernheim was genuinely delighted to hear about his important meetings. He was as much in love with these harmless deceptions as anyone, and he used them for fear that he should be the victim of a similar lie himself. For this reason he said:

'Call Mr Robinson, tell him I'm in an important meeting, and ask him to drop round tomorrow.'

'Mr Robinson asks you,' said the secretary, having made the call, 'to go to see him. He is busy all day tomorrow.'

'Then let him wait!' said Bernheim with a show of

irritation. Robinson's reply annoyed him, but still more annoying was the fact that he had failed to see it coming. He wanted to give some more instructions, but superstition had caught him. Everything will go wrong today!

He was getting up to go. There was another ring.

'Your brother,' said the secretary.

'Is that you, Theodor?' asked Paul.

'Yes,' said Theodor. 'Stay where you are, I'll be with you in five minutes.'

Theodor arrived.

For the first time in many months he was wearing civilian clothes. The brown shirts were mouldering at home. He turned down Paul's invitation to sit. He stood in the winter twilight, a few stars of snow quickly fading away into his coat, and held his hat in his hand – he might as well have held it like a supplicant, in both. Humiliated, in his brother's apartment. Paul was even more a stranger to him, surrounded by strange furniture, between walls that were Paul's and Paul's only. It was not his mother's house, where Theodor could still enjoy the feeling of being disinherited, a lofty bitterness that itself confers a kind of ownership. Will he help me? Up until the moment when he had pressed Paul's doorbell, he had had no precise plan. He had been quite unable to imagine a remark he might open with, or what Paul might say in reply. Now he could think of nothing at all. Dusk was falling in the room. Paul didn't switch on the light. It was as though he was invoking the darkening heavens for help against Theodor.

Before it gets completely dark I'll say it, thought Theodor.

Finally he blurted out, 'I need at least two thousand dollars right away!'

'I haven't got it.'

'I have to leave tonight. With Gustav. You don't know him. He's done a job.'

'What are you telling me? Are you anything to do with it?'

'You can hand me over to the police if you like. I'm involved.' And because it suddenly occurred to him that Paul might think him a common criminal, he added quickly:

'It's political.'

The word continued to ring in Paul's ears. Night had fallen. Again Paul remembered Nikita.

'I've got no money.'

'Telephone, borrow, hurry, right away!' Theodor started, loudly now, as though, seeing that night had fallen, there was no point in being cautious any more.

'And what,' asked Paul slowly, 'if I don't give you any money?'

'You – ' screamed Theodor. He grabbed at the table, and a glass paperweight slid into his hand. He hurled it to the floor. It crashed.

At that moment the doorbell rang. Paul answered it.

In stepped Nikolai Brandeis.

He was a powerful, well-built man in his forties, with surprisingly supple, feline movements and a low, gentle voice, whose charm lay in the strange foreign inflection it put on words. At times it seemed that Brandeis mispronounced syllables on purpose. Those who knew him were surprised by the speed and range of his intelligence, and puzzled by the insistency with which he kept to his old mistakes. He had the impolite habit of repeating the sentence that had just been addressed to him, in his own rhythm and with his own errors, as though to correct the speaker, or perhaps to confirm that he had understood him correctly. This habit made people suspicious of him. If people dislike having their mistakes corrected, then how much more irritating it is when even their correctness is not allowed to stand. Brandeis was alien to them. They were only able to tolerate a certain amount of strangeness, and Brandeis overdid it. In an illustrated atlas, as a harmless museum exhibit, he might have been thought to be 'exotic'. Brandeis, though, was alive.

He appeared to be descended from some obscure strain of titanic, heavy-boned Mongols. His black pointed beard brought his broad, heart-shaped face to such a resounding conclusion that it looked stuck on, and since his upper lip was clean shaven, one genuinely believed for a moment that Brandeis had forgotten to take the beard off after some fancy dress party. His narrow, slanting eyes were a surprising pale grey. And, astonishingly, over this triangular face, and contrasting with its yellow-brown tinge, there rose a high, broad, white forehead that was surely someone else's. Only the thin matt-black hair that hung down in a few strands bore some relation to the face, the beard and the slanting eyes.

All that was known of this striking looking man was that, in common with thousands of others, he had left Russia at the time of the Revolution. Since he could point to no family, no relatives and no friends, since he'd made no friends during his time in Berlin, and associated neither with foreigners nor with natives, only transacted business, and business of every kind at that, people began to notice him, and to suspect him of some criminality or other. He quickly became known. Dislike and suspicion make a man more conspicuous than love and affection. No one who had ever seen him could forget him. They fell for the melancholic charm of his voice, and suspected that he must harbour some secret.

One might run into him in banks and in boardrooms, in the stock exchange, in the cafés of the business district. One happened to know that he lived at a small pension in the west of the city, but did not take his meals there. Occasionally one might see him at an advanced hour in one of the private gaming clubs. He would sit in a corner, drink up, pay and leave. The bars were closed, the gaming clubs were merely their surrogates as far as he was concerned. He accepted no invitations. He walked everywhere. Of all the people with whom he did business, he was the only one not to have a car, and, curiously, the only one who was never in a hurry. One might see him walking down the street with powerful strides, but slowly, provocatively slowly, a metal-tipped cane pointing up at the sky like a shouldered rifle, the hand holding it buried in his coat-pocket, and his narrow-brimmed hat pulled down over his eyes. Thus girded, he had the self-confidence of a man walking at the head of a great band of followers.

Some months previously, he had brought off a major transaction with Paul Bernheim. Several hundred field-kitchens, old and in poor condition, stored at a depot in the

Steiermark, about which the Austrian state didn't concern itself because it wasn't sufficiently alert, and because the things came under the purview of the Allied Weapons' Commission, were to be sold off as scrap metal to Yugoslavia. But the buyer wanted an Austrian company to supply him. Brandeis offered a 30 per cent profit if Bernheim's bank would take on the role of buyer in the Steiermark and seller to the Yugoslavs. The purchase price was low, and Brandeis himself would be responsible for bribing the district commissioner and a treasury official. There was almost no risk for Bernheim. When the transaction had gone through, Bernheim was astonished to receive 45 per cent from Brandeis, not the agreed thirty. Paul feared a trap and returned 15 per cent to Brandeis. He received a letter in which Brandeis apologised for the mistake, putting it down to a book-keeping error.

Since that time, Bernheim had heard nothing from Brandeis. His sudden appearance on this day, after hours, and just when Paul's brother was paying an unexpected visit, deepened the man's mystery and Paul's apprehension. What was Brandeis after? Did he know about Theodor? Was he in cahoots with the police? Were they both in danger?

For some seconds, Paul was unable to say anything. He stood with his hand on the door-latch, which he had closed on Brandeis' entry, as though he meant to leave the premises to him. Brandeis' cane was lowered, perhaps in recognition of the fact that he was indoors, though his hat stayed on. He waited. Finally, as Paul still didn't say anything, he said:

'You have a visitor, and I'm disturbing you. It's probably best I should go.'

Theodor in the meantime had switched a light on. He was sitting in a large armchair, thin and pale and cold. When Brandeis nodded to him curtly, Theodor only lowered his eyes.

Paul had hoped the stranger's arrival would drive his brother away, but then Theodor broke the silence:

'When can I have the money?'

'It's not possible – ' began Paul.

Theodor rose to his feet quickly, with his upper body leaning forward, and without taking his hands out of his pockets. His movement was like a threatening and venomous reply from his whole twisted body.

At that moment Brandeis said: 'How much is it you need, young Herr Bernheim?'

'My brother wanted two thousand dollars, but I can't lay my hands on it at the moment. You understand, at this time of night,' said Paul.

'May I help you out?' asked Brandeis. He pulled out a roll of dollar bills with an elastic band round them. He counted out two thousand in hundreds and gave them to Paul. Brandeis had counted so quickly that only seconds seemed to have passed between his question and the moment when he slipped the elastic band round the remaining money.

Without a word – in fact as if he'd been mute for decades – Paul handed his brother the money.

Theodor nodded. Paul followed him out into the hall. Before Theodor could reach it, Paul had opened the front door. The brothers didn't shake hands. Theodor left.

Slowly, Paul closed the door after him. When he turned round, he caught sight of Brandeis in the hall mirror. He must have witnessed their goodbye.

'I thank you,' began Paul. 'Tomorrow I'll – '

'There's no hurry,' interrupted the soft voice. 'We have some bigger business ahead of us, if you're interested. As you see, I have money, and cash at that.'

'Quite frankly,' said Paul, 'if you hadn't come, I wouldn't have given him anything.'

'You'd have been wrong, then. Do you want to deliver the young man to the hands of the police?'

'How – ' blurted Paul.

' – do I know? I don't. But, consider, a young man, in these times, wanting money, in the evening, straight away, and a substantial sum. I know young people. Their emotions are more expensive than ours were, or yours too. What did we want? Women. Today's youth wants blood. And that's without price.'

'And you understand that?'

'Of course I do! I understand that these people are drawn to death as we once were to life. They fear death as we used to fear life, and they long for it as we used to long for life. Don't imagine that it's these so-called pernicious ideas that are motivating the young people of today. They are motivated by fear and thirst, like animals. The ideas are pretexts – always were.' The voice grew softer and softer. Brandeis put his hand on the table and played on it as on a keyboard. 'Ideas are pretexts, there are always ideas. I will open the door to let in a dog barking outside at night – excuse the comparison – and I will give your brother money so that he can get away. I realise, though,

85

that I am not doing him a favour. Because, you see, the dog has a home and a master and a dog's shape. But this young man will find himself in front of many locked doors, and since he has a human shape, no one will let him in. These people are so unhappy! They have no joys left, only ideals. How sad idealists are!

'But let's get back to business! Lest I appear too noble to you, I will confess that I only produce money so swiftly when I need someone. I need you! As you know, I'm a stranger in this city. People here don't trust me. I do everything I can to make them suspicious of me. Now, an elementary transaction. I have cloth. Very good quality, cheap, but unfortunately in a bright blue that isn't worn. I could wait for the fashion to change, certainly. But waiting! I made enquiries. I could dye the cloth, but that makes it stiff. There is only one possible use for it. In uniforms!' Brandeis paused. He waited for Paul to concur. Paul said nothing.

'I'm looking for someone,' Brandeis resumed, 'to supply the authorities, customs and excise, police, with cloth.'

'I'll see what I can do,' said Paul.

'You yourself will be that supplier,' said Brandeis. He buttoned up his coat, which he had kept on, reached for his cane, which had been resting against his chair like a living being, and stood up. He seemed taller to Paul, as though he had grown while sitting. Bernheim's eyes were only level with the tip of the great man's beard.

8

Theodor vanished.

He had taken a hasty leave of his mother, and a thorough one of his room. As he emptied his drawers, burned his papers, unloaded his pistols and stowed them and the rapiers away in stiff linen umbrella covers, he had felt extraordinarily close to tears. He dreaded the prospect of staying on the farm of a Hungarian sympathiser, he dreaded the countryside, which he thought of as dirty and backward, he dreaded the unfamiliar pharmacies where unscrupulous chemists would confuse sleeping-draughts and fever remedies, the inadequate opticians who were guaranteed not to understand his two-and-a-half dioptres, and finally he dreaded being poor. His mother and Paul were quite capable of leaving him to starve in that foreign place. Gustav, who had been responsible for the whole thing, was the poor son of a cottager, and staying on the property of a Hungarian magnate would be like a holiday as far as he was concerned. Carefully Theodor packed his pyjamas and his twenty-four ties. He regretted having asked Paul for only two thousand dollars. He should have asked for four. Gustav's whistle might sound at any moment. True to the principles of their society, they had agreed on a whistle as

87

a signal, even for the hour of their flight. Conspirators whistled, didn't they?

And Gustav's whistle came, mercilessly. Theodor shut his suitcase and had the porter carry it, but only as far as the gate. Gustav mustn't laugh at him and think him a traitor. Theodor would lug the suitcase from the gate to the car waiting at the corner by himself. Gustav was already in the car. Theodor sighed. Gustav made no move. Theodor had hoped his comrade might lift the suitcase into the car for him.

'It's easy for you,' said Theodor. 'You're much stronger than I am.' But Gustav showed no trace of compassion for him. All the way to the station, Theodor kept up a bitter silence.

Frau Bernheim was sitting over some needlework in the cold dining room and crying when Paul arrived. For her, tears had ceased to be the result of a particular stimulus. Rather, as with many older women, they had become a mere habit of the eyes. She would cry for some time before even realising it; her tears flowed like rain in the country, steady, thin and comforting. Her grief was soluble in water. It would always flow from the inflamed eyes, down the same two furrows between cheeks and nose, and down from the corners of the mouth into two other furrows that divided the broad chin from the cheeks. Then the tears would lose themselves in the folds of the old throat, and in the high collar of her black dress, kept up as ever by its unrelenting whalebone.

'You're not to cry, mother!' said Paul.

'I'm not,' replied Frau Bernheim, 'it just comes over me like this sometimes.' They sat in silence in the dining room for three hours after supper and froze. Frau Bernheim had an old plaid of her husband's wrapped round her legs. Her ivory knitting-needles chattered like teeth. The windows shook in the wind. A chill from the garden beat against the house.

'You want some company, mother.'

'Yes, I've thought of that. And now Theodor's gone, I thought of his room. You know it has its own separate entrance from the hall.'

'What do you mean?'

'Well, we can't simply pin a notice on the door or put an advertisement in the newspapers, so I asked Herr Merwig to make some discreet enquiries for a single lady of good background, and she would have to pay something, yes, she would have to pay. Together, the two of us could afford to keep on the maid. Otherwise I'd have to get rid of her. I'd have good cause, too. Just lately there was money missing from the charity tin, and I thought she might have taken it. Why not? Servants are honest for three years, then they start filching. But you can't find any better nowadays. And so I'd keep her on if I had a little more money coming in. I'm pleased with Merwig, he's going about it very discreetly, and there's someone coming tomorrow, a lady whose husband worked in the Defence Ministry.'

Frau Hammer moved into Theodor's room.

Henceforth the two women would sit in the dining room every evening, and freeze and crochet and look up suspiciously now and again, and go on crocheting. Whenever she came into the dining room, Frau Bernheim would say, 'Excuse me a moment,' and go into the corridor. She went 'to have a look at Theodor's room', because she had noticed that her tenant was apt to be forgetful and leave the light on there. But she never breathed a word to Frau Hammer. It was a joy for her to go and see for herself, and to economise with her own hands.

The other woman's presence bothered Paul. His visits grew less frequent. His mother may have exaggerated, but they really weren't even well-to-do any more. Already, unbeknown to her, Paul had had to take out two mortgages on the house. And still there was no prospect of becoming rich – unless through that business with the cloth that Brandeis had suggested to him. Could Brandeis be trusted? Of course, one wasn't prejudiced, but wasn't there something rather sinister about these people from the east? One didn't exactly have to believe in the seven wise men of Zion. But didn't people from the east have a different set of morals, didn't they act in accordance with some occult eastern wisdom? They knew secrets and they would act on them. Did honour matter to Brandeis? Brandeis wasn't afraid of prison. But Paul? Didn't he have his whole life ahead of him?

He felt in the mood for another talk with Dr König, whose resistance always provided a spur to Paul's ambition. He asked him to dinner at Hessler's. Ah, good restaurants! When Paul stepped into a good restaurant, he no longer had doubts about his career. Everything here confirmed his hopes. The conscientiousness of the waiter and the optimistic gleam of the lamps, the diners plying knife and fork, the healthy complexion of the ladies, even the cripples begging outside the door, and the freezing policeman who shooed them away, and who seemed not like an official of the state, but an employee of the diners. He wasn't acting in the name of the law, but in accordance with the wishes of the manager, the doorman, the violinist and Paul himself. If one had the money, one might keep him forever, the whole power of the law at one's gates, night and day. In this restaurant, especially when one brought along a revolutionary as one's guest – making him doubly rebarbative – one forgot one's doubts. It was as though the ease with which the diners spent their money bred in Paul the notion that it was as easy to acquire it. A woman smiled, and it was comforting to know one could still afford a night with her. The cigarette girl offered herself along with a packet of Amenophis cork filters, and it was wonderful to know one had enough money for 365 nights of cigarette girl. Soon he would have enough money for years of the wives of dye manufacturers. There they sat, the poison-gas moguls, and one was almost their equal. Did they have any inkling of the fact that, compared to them, one was a pauper? No! They had not! Nor was one a pauper. One was simply on the way up, not yet arrived.

For political reasons, Dr König wasn't wearing a dinner jacket but a dark suit: as though one might mount a challenge to capitalist society by turning up in a dark suit. He didn't realise it, but it showed off Paul's English dinner jacket to superb advantage, and Paul would have been dismayed had König worn a dinner jacket. After his third glass of wine, Dr König underwent a revolution compared to which the one in Russia was a tea party. Dr König saw himself in power. He wondered how, without impairing his conscience, he might take the poor, ruined Paul Bernheim – now a streetsweeper, and lucky to be that! – into his protection. As if from many miles away, he heard Paul's lengthy expatiation. Talk all you like! thought König, while Paul, in love with his dinner jacket, his gestures, and the sound of his own voice, was extolling the stock exchange. 'That's my terrain,' he said. 'When I'm there I feel the way you do when you address the masses. I just love the inhuman frenzy of it, those voices that belong to insects, not human beings. The blackboards, the quick dab of the sponge that wipes everything away, and the even quicker chalk that writes up the new numbers. Oh, how I love it: going to the telephone and praying for a quick connection to my secretary. I telephone, I hurry back, and the new numbers prove me right. You have to have a feel for it! A quick word with the bank, and then fifty in the convertible to get up an appetite for dinner. That's what I call living!'

'Tell me,' said Dr König, who thought the drink had gone to Paul Bernheim's head, and hoped to get something of real significance out of him, 'what do you make of what's going on in the Ruhrgebiet?'

'As I see it,' replied Paul, who had no intention of disappointing the revolutionary, 'and going by what my friends tell me, both sides are behaving equally stupidly. France is almost worse than we are, and we're bad enough. But that's the way it is. So long as those idiotic politicians behave as though it was still 1900, and don't hand over control to the industrialists, there'll be trouble in Europe. I think that's something you and I are agreed on: that economics should govern politics.' And, to prove that he had an equal mastery of extra-Continental affairs, he added: 'They sorted that out some time ago in England!'

'You're well up on England, aren't you,' observed Dr König flatteringly.

Since Paul had by now finished his sixth glass, he responded unhesitatingly: 'A second home to me, really. You know the major part of my education was at Oxford. They were good times, then the war came along.' Paul seemed to have forgotten that he had actually left England before the war began. 'I'd love to go back there before it's really too late. You know, Dr König, you understand me pretty well, and you know about my intellectual pursuits, but the things I'm most proud of are the two pots I won for rowing at Oxford. I'll show them to you next time you come round.'

Of all the restaurant ceremonies, paying was the one Paul liked best. He loved the discreet nod to the waiter and the folded bill laid confidingly before him. Sometimes he thought it proper to check it. Sometimes he was content merely to glance at the total. From his seat he gauged the depth of the waiter's bow behind him. He never talked to waiters, unlike Dr König, who as a man of the people felt it incumbent upon him to say 'Goodnight!' loudly and class-consciously.

Once outside and sobered up by the cold air, Bernheim was afraid of what he had divulged. He clung silently to Dr König, and suggested a visit to the gaming club. With panic in his heart, he tried to crack a joke, to play the kindly, cheerful, carefree, worldly host. But already he was thinking: I'm going to fall for that damned Brandeis after all. I need money, I have to get rich. Maybe I'll win big tonight.

Yes, he seriously believed that one day he would have a really big win at the gaming club. Waving to the pale, scrawny lookout posted at the corner and blue with cold, he felt a new surge of hope. The sight of that wretch warmed his heart. Hard, bare, yellow scabs of leather showed where his narrow fur collar had gone bald. His trousers were far too short for his skinny legs, his boots rattled in the cold like chattering teeth, and all this proved to Paul Bernheim the splendour of his own position. In the squeak of the door that led to the mysterious corridor he heard the future calling, and he saw the porter's romantic lantern as a symbolic light. Commonsense wanted to expose the feebleness of the whole masquerade, but he told it to be quiet. He was going to win a fortune. He didn't want to be woken.

But upstairs in the gaming rooms, where smoke shrouded the walls, ceilings and lamps, and the smell of the middle-class life that the flat's occupants led in the daytime fought against the nocturnal smell of vice, Paul lost the heart to gamble. It wasn't that the cards were against him – they obeyed him, but in moderation, keeping as it were a decent, respectful distance from him. Although he knew all the rooms, he always forgot them before coming here. Outside on the pavement he hoped they might have miraculously changed since the night before. How rapturously he might have gambled if, instead of the motley crowd of film extras, private tutors, freelance journalists and other scroungers, only wealthy men had been sitting at the tables, as in England. The moment he showed his face in here, his friends would come rushing up to him for a loan. He had long since acquired the ability to lie about money, and his feigned embarrassment at being momentarily impecunious was readily credited. But it meant he couldn't gamble any large sums – and what he won with small stakes went straight into the pockets of his friends. The prints on the walls bothered him, the knick-knacks in glass cabinets, the imitation Persian rugs, the antimacassars on the chairs – all the décor betrayed the flat's petty-bourgeois mustiness, the husband's respectable job, and his wife's altered clothes. Sometimes one would come upon a locked door behind a portière, and hear some member of the family snoring behind it. The son of the house was posted in the corridor in case the police raided, his sister was making black coffee in the kitchen. A yawning waiter shuffled between the tables in a spectral pair of tails. How could one challenge destiny under such circumstances?

But, come midnight, Paul was always to be found in a gaming club. The solitude of his flat was insufferable. He had been longing for a change for months now. In the constant expectation of being caught gambling by the police, he had stopped carrying his identity papers with him. The police duly struck. He was loaded into a van with the others, and kept at the police station till morning. One night stolen from solitude! He saw the pale dawn tinge the office room, the ancient dust on the green labels on the index files, the scabby, cracked and sweating walls, and the yellow stain of the nightlight, which by order had to remain on until 8 o'clock. Then he passed through the warren of offices. He stopped in front of the case displaying photographs of unidentified corpses, and looked at the faces of the dead, disfigured by horrible wounds, crushed skulls, ripped eyelids, slashed mouths, ears gnawed away by rats. So many people quit this life – and no one even knew who they were.

'A pleasant family album, wouldn't you say?' said a voice behind him. It was Nikolai Brandeis.

'Did they scoop you up too?' asked Paul.

'No, I've come here of my own accord. Maybe not entirely of my own accord,' said Brandeis. 'I quite often have business here. I can assure you I don't enjoy it. But I'm in the habit of looking at the pictures of the unclaimed corpses before going on to one of the police offices. I find it comforting, you see. Encouraging. Who would have thought there were so many people whom no one misses? You could work out how many similar people are still alive, perhaps. They stagger along the city pavements, and death is stalking them, death . . . But now I feel refreshed. Would you care to accompany me where I'm going? I need a visa.'

Brandeis needed a visa in order to go to Latvia, where he had some old business associates. As a refugee who had fled without documents, he was still registered as stateless, and that made travelling complicated.

'If you come with me,' said Brandeis, 'you'll observe there's not much difference between my status and that of the people in the photographs. Come along.'

The official sat behind a wooden partition, and like policemen the world over, he was a devotee of overheated rooms. As a member of the immigration police, he hated immigrants. When Brandeis said, 'Good morning,' the official replied, 'What do you want?'

'To wish you a good morning,' said Brandeis. 'Also an exit and re-entry visa.'

'You don't have a residence permit!'

'I've applied for one. It hasn't come through yet.'

'In that case you'll be able to leave, but not come back.'

'You see if I don't!' said Brandeis in a whisper, as though it was a secret.

It is a characteristic of officialdom only to look at the applicant before it after three or four sentences, as though it assumed that all foreigners looked alike, and having seen one meant one could easily imagine all the others. The policeman now looked up. He saw the powerful frame of Brandeis in his black coat with the collar turned up. He stood up, as though to reduce the difference in height between himself and the foreigner. He wanted to say something. Suddenly Brandeis said loudly: 'Herr Kampe, isn't it? I'll be back in three hours from now.' He pointed at the office clock with his stick. 'Good day.'

'You see,' he said to Bernheim, 'and in three hours I'll have my visa. Just because I knew his name, which wasn't difficult to find out. He probably hasn't done anything wrong. But because I said his name, he's afraid I might have some dirt on him. No one is without blemish.'

'And if he refuses to give you a visa?' asked Bernheim.

Brandeis pulled out a Danish passport. 'Then I'll use this.'

'Is it forged?'

'Depends,' replied Brandeis. 'What in this world is real anyway? Did you think about the cloth?'

'Ah, the money, Herr Brandeis –'

'No, not the money,' Brandeis interrupted, 'the cloth!' And he swung his stick towards the heavens, said goodbye, and left Bernheim standing.

His sleepless night, the photographs he'd seen, Brandeis' conversation with the official, the recollection of his business proposal, the money and Theodor: they all bewildered Paul Bernheim. The mightier Brandeis appeared to him, the feebler he himself felt. The square lay buried in snow that had fallen overnight, and that hadn't yet lost its whiteness to the traffic. The street traders shouted their wares, the overground trains thundered, the lorries rattled. It was the first time Paul Bernheim had visited this area in the early morning. Previously he had only seen it on mild, consoling winter afternoons; the golden lights of the big department store, the shops, the underground. Now that he could take in the entire square, it seemed to have been created by some brutal will; in spite of the white snow, one could feel the shadow of the powerful, maroon-clad police, and the department store, so close in the evening with its lights on, seemed now a long way off, among the uniform white of the houses. There was some connection between this square and the pictures of the unidentified corpses at the police station. He hurried down the stairs, as though the underground wasn't merely a form of transport, but a warm, subterranean refuge. For the first time in months, he rode on the crowded underground. Every face recalled one of the dead. When he got home, he went to bed.

Normally sleep could be relied upon to dispel the terrors of the day, and the introduction of an artificially created night would present Bernheim with a new and transformed day when he woke. But today the charm failed to work. When he rose, he found waiting for him one of his mother's thick letters that always contained some disagreeable news. For since Frau Bernheim had begun to economise on postage, she only wrote on particularly dire occasions, and then at great length, so as to get full value from stamps and writing paper.

His mother's letter enclosed another one, from Theodor. He needed money. If Paul Bernheim had had a slighter better memory at this point, he would surely have noticed the similarity between Theodor's epistolary style and his own in his Oxford days. 'Dear Mama!' wrote Theodor, 'urgently require monnaie. Healthy life, fresh air, assumed name. Wonderful hospitality. – Often think of you and Paul, but no time for exchange of views. Need monnaie urgently. Try sending by wire! Post slow in these parts. Hugs. Your son Theodor.'

Frau Bernheim wrote a tremulous letter to accompany this. The longer Theodor was away, and the more rarely she heard any news of him by the cautious roundabout methods that had to be employed, the more noble, unfortunate and deserving of help he seemed to her. Yes, she, who in his presence had viewed his friends, his secretive outings and train journeys, his leaflets and newspapers with fear and apprehension, now began to see 'the government' as a personal enemy, and to blame 'the Jews' for Theodor's 'misfortune' – which was how she referred to his flight. 'He's suffering for his political beliefs!' Her maternal vanity had come up with the phrase one day. Even so, when Paul replied that he could not give any more money to Theodor, on whose account he had already run up a large debt, and surely it was a simple matter to transfer the rent for Theodor's room to Hungary once a month, Frau Bernheim replied indignantly that she would not contemplate making any further sacrifices for her children. 'I sacrificed my entire youth for you,' she wrote. She really believed that, but for her sons, she should have grown old far more slowly. Blood was thicker than water, she added, and one should help one's own brother.

In the meantime, she herself was saving up for her old age. She had a suitcase full of banknotes that were growing more worthless by the day, but in whose value she had an unshakeable faith. The endeavours of Paul and Merwig were in vain. Since she had been proved right in the matter of war bonds, she believed in her 'financial instinct', as she called it. Whenever Paul came home, she would ask him for a few notes. 'That'll just about get you a newspaper!' Paul would say. She smoothed them down, went over to her suitcase and laid them with the others.

One day Paul woke up determined to risk the deal with Brandeis. He telephoned his hotel but was told that Brandeis had gone away. He would be back in a week. Paul waited. So as not to lose courage, he repeated to himself every day: 'I must get rich.' Finally Brandeis was back. They met.

'About the money,' Brandeis began, 'there's no rush, Herr Bernheim!'

'No,' said Paul, 'I want to talk about the cloth.'

'It's too late,' said Brandeis. 'I've sold it. You must admit I did ask you one last time before I left.'

'Oh yes, but very fleetingly. You hardly mentioned it.'

'I didn't want to appear insistent, Herr Bernheim. A quality that is often ascribed to us.'

They were sitting in a café. Brandeis examined the walls, which were covered by excrescences, an affliction of the plasterwork, a prismatic version of the plague of boils, the thickly veiled standard lamps in niches, where the naked octahedral nymphs of modern design were leaning. 'So that's the style they build in nowadays!' he said. He seemed to have forgotten why Paul had come to see him.

Bernheim wanted to take up the subject again. 'Don't let's talk about that, it's gone,' said Brandeis. 'I bear you no ill will. Perhaps you were right. I haven't got any money back on it yet. I'm afraid I may have to board a train again. Get another visa – '

When the evening papers appeared with the closing prices, Bernheim noticed that Brandeis showed no interest in them.

'You're surprised?' said Brandeis. 'Yesterday I sold everything.'

'And?'

'Got into dollars.' Before they parted, he said: 'I should sell too, Herr Bernheim.'

But Bernheim didn't sell.

Part Two

9

Spring came suddenly that year.

The rooms were still redolent of the cold and gloom of winter. The windows were flung open. The houses seemed like opened tombs, and the people approaching the windows resembled amiable yellow corpses. The barrel-organs too had been resurrected, and they flocked in the courtyards as though they had returned with the migrating birds from the south, and their sound made even the sceptics more cheerful. Extremist demonstrations in the streets became more frequent. Politics flourished in the friendly beams of the young sun, and under the nourishing rain of the mild, veiled nights.

On one particular Sunday morning of that spring, a tall, strikingly powerful man could be seen making his way extremely slowly among the contented strollers on the Kurfürstendamm. Brandeis was still wearing his coat, and had the collar turned up. People turned to stare at him. He seemed quite unconcerned by the pedestrians, whom he mostly dwarfed anyway. His slant eyes took in the houses, the names of the businesses, the

105

displays in the shop windows, the trees lining the road, the traffic, and the kiosks closed for Sunday and resembling boarded-up, deconsecrated churches. His Mongol features and brownish complexion were sufficient for the central Europeans passing him to classify him as 'Oriental', along with Buddhas, geishas and opium addicts. Since the inflation was now over, and people's morale, patriotism and confidence were all boosted by a sense of the value of their currency, the stranger was viewed with rather more suspicion than wonder.

People were strolling along in the sunshine, in their spring fashions, when all at once there was a vague commotion. It began, like the wind before a storm, at a particular street corner, far away. A few people started running. Others stopped and looked around, evidently trying to combine personal safety with dignity. The noise was growing more distinct all the time. You could distinguish the singing voices of massed columns of men, the massed tramping of hobnailed boots on asphalt. And then, above the singing and the metallic pounding of marching feet, you could hear reedy, wheedling flutes, the piping of abstract, disembodied music, playing a popular marching tune. Finally one could see what caused these sounds: a few cyclists wobbling about as an advance guard, and behind them the first rows of marching men, men with moustaches that put one in mind of decency and proud fatherhood, with open, unseeing eyes – eyes in which outrage, rectitude and pride had overpowered the faculty of sight – with swinging arms that were like empty sleeves, and with canes fastened to their belts to indicate that they were something more than merely walking-sticks. They were somewhere on the evolutionary path from cudgel to sabre.

The majority of the pedestrians had vanished down the sidestreets. The rattle of closing shutters could be heard from all the houses. Presently, the sun was shining on dusty, deserted cobbles. The pedestrians were now hurrying away towards their homes in Grunewald. In reply to the irregular pattering of their feet came the implacable thud of nailed boots on the main street. The singing now reached above the treetops. The spectral flutes pierced the clanging of the noonday bells which, to add to the confusion, were just getting going, announcing divine retribution, the end of the world, and the approach of those who would destroy it. It was a real Sunday, a Sunday of the kind that are sometimes visited upon German cities: solemn, fervent and awful.

Among the handful of men who had stopped to watch the procession was Brandeis. He stood next to a pissoir, a commodity which in Berlin is rarer than a library. He smiled. One could be forgiven for thinking that the reason he stood there wasn't to indulge his own curiosity, but rather that of everyone else, as if it were his duty to show marchers and runners alike how to stand one's ground; to show the unseeing how to look; the agitated how to be calm; the politicians how to think; the idealists how to question. Yes, and however outlandish he appeared, and even though he kept his coat on, oblivious of the sun, there was still a connection between him and the aspiring treetops, and the breezy, balmy spring air. Between the marchers and the spring there was none. Even if one knew for a fact that they were marching into a

107

wood, the impression they gave was rather that they were marching against it.

Although his mother had come to his Jewish father from a Protestant parsonage, and brought with her a Luther Bible, a mandolin and a subscription to a family periodical, Nikolai Brandeis did not feel at home in Germany. He felt rather as though the little German settlement in the Ukraine had been a truer version of Germany than the country itself, from which successive emigrants carry away what is native, while successive immigrants bring in what is alien. The bound volumes of the magazine his mother kept painted a misleading picture. They represented the country as it might perhaps have been at the time when the settlers left it. At home, Brandeis could remember, in spite of having inherited his father's physiognomy, he had been accepted among the Swabian faces of his playmates, been one of them. But here, where people's faces gave no indication of belonging to any particular race – Brandeis referred to them as asphalt Slavs – here he was a stranger. Only the hesitancy of early spring reminded him of the shy and frugal bounty of his home.

He remembered his boyhood. His father, whom he had lost at a relatively young age, and who had probably been just such a bashful nature-lover as he himself was. His father had wanted to convert to Greek Orthodoxy, in order to escape the constraints under which Jews had to live in Old Russia. And because converted Jews were made to declare their previous faith, he intended, like many another, to become first Lutheran, and then Orthodox. But even a man who conducts his relationships with

God and State on such a practical basis may fall victim to a weakness one might not have credited in him. Old Brandeis, going to the Lutheran pastor to deceive him, was met by divine punishment before he could even fulfil his purpose: he fell in love with the pastor's daughter. Perhaps he only had it in mind to seduce her in time-honoured fashion, and not marry her at all. But if that were the case, he failed to reckon with her virtue.

So he married. He stayed in the settlement. He never did become Orthodox. He abandoned his great plans and became a small shopkeeper with a bit of land, a gentle wife, and a father-in-law who was a parson. After a year, Nikolai was born, or, to give him his full name, Friedrich Theodor Emmanuel Nikolai. His father had added the Russian name as an afterthought, in the secret hope that the boy might one day achieve some eminence in Russia, something for which the Nikolai might come in handy. He never stopped thinking practically, old Brandeis, in the manner of his tribe. He died suddenly, in a typhoid epidemic. But he left enough money to pay for his son to have an education.

Nikolai's studies were interrupted by the Russo-Japanese War, from which he returned as an officer in the 106th Infantry. He thought about becoming a career soldier. While at university, he had never associated with the zealots. He had never understood their ideals. Reactionaries, liberals and revolutionaries alike all left him cold. One might have thought he wasn't a true Russian. Since his youngest days he had been taciturn and distrustful of talk. Of all Russian institutions, the army seemed to him the safest bet. There, too, there was politicking, but at least in a crisis, he thought, discipline would thrust politics aside. Army rules were banal, but they were rules: rifle drill, exercise grounds, recruits and barracks, the Tsar's portrait, medals and commendations, that was all clear and unambiguous. The civil service meant finding a protector, becoming involved in intrigues, and politicking on top of that. To become a businessman – well, he didn't have the capital. He had studied mathematics, and thought his gifts might qualify him for the Engineers.

But his mother, who was old by now and had inherited a little money from her father, and was farming a few acres, beseeched him to go to Germany and study.

She was afraid of further wars. Simple soul that she was, she believed that within a year Russia would go looking for revenge on Japan. Nikolai complied. He studied at several German universities, read economics rather than mathematics, was bored and lonely, returned to his mother, helped at home, and finally, out of sheer indifference, became a schoolteacher in his native village of Helenental.

He led a simple and quiet life, ate and drank regularly, had no time for women, went to the Crimea for a fortnight's holiday, hurried home for the harvest, read a lot, was fond of his pupils, gathered dogs about himself and every so often played cards with a group of local officials. In 1913 his mother died. The following year he went to war for a second time, and by 1917 he was a captain. When the first revolution broke out, he supported it. He fought the Bolsheviks, was captured by them, and went over to their side. With all the confusion around him, that decision was something stable, and it would surely help put his life onto an even keel.

But he had miscalculated. One day there took place one of those episodes – at once typical and insignificant in the general scheme of the revolutionary wars – that are capable of turning a man's life, principles and decisions upside down. Now it was Nikolai Brandeis' turn to make the discovery that, in the space of a single hour, which can seem anything but decisive at the time – a man is capable of so completely changing what is described as 'his character' that he might well look in the mirror to see whether he still has the same face. Ever since that transformation in his life, Brandeis would insist that experience doesn't mature people, it changes their natures. He remembered the lunatic in his village at home, who never tired of asking everyone he met: 'How many are you? Are you *one*?' No, one wasn't just *one*. One was ten people, twenty, a hundred. The more opportunities life gave us, the more beings it revealed in us. A man might die because he hadn't experienced anything, and had been just *one* person all his life.

To return to the event in question: after fighting in the Ukraine for a time, Brandeis was posted to his native district, and put in charge of a group of German settlements he knew well. He had orders to supervise the immediate redistribution of all movable and immovable property among the inhabitants of the settlements. It was one of the many wrong-headed, capricious, and pathologically inspired decrees of those times. These German settlements were perhaps the only villages in Russia where the primitive idea of redistribution – which the peasants elsewhere were only too quick to grasp – was apparently not understood. Nikolai Brandeis himself had no opinion on the pros and cons of the measure. But, in accordance with his resolution to be a simple soldier and nothing more, and to enjoy the luxury of obedience as he might enjoy a holiday, he took the measures he was required to take, and simply began driving surplus cows from the stalls of the richer farmers into those of the poorer ones – to the anger of the inhabitants, who were the more irate because they had known him for so long. He called a meeting, and explained that this was a foretaste of the coming age, and was the express wish of the new government. He was heard in silence. Then he went along to the next village to do the same thing. And then to a third. But when he returned to the first village, it transpired that the poor farmers had of their own accord returned the cattle of their richer neighbours. Once more, their stalls were empty. They had no intention of keeping what they referred to as 'others' property'.

Nikolai Brandeis reported what had happened, and was given a reprimand and told to use force if necessary. He threatened the settlers with imprisonment and deportation. It made no difference. A commissar came and arrested the parson, a man Brandeis had known well for years. Brandeis petitioned for the old man to be released, but instead he was sentenced to death. Brandeis commanded the firing squad. With the whole village present, he gave the order 'Fire!'

When the echo of the shots had rolled away, uncertainty crept into Brandeis' heart for the first time. So far, he had always acted like a professional soldier, with unquestioning obedience. But now, with the body of the parson, who had died kneeling, slumped in front of the blue washed wall, the wall that Nikolai had so often straddled as a little boy, and the dark red pool of blood growing tentatively in size, and sending out one or two rivulets over the uneven ground between the stones – at that moment Brandeis changed. In front of everyone in the village, he took off his cap, and he bowed to the dead man. Then he gave instructions for him to be buried in the churchyard, went to the commissar and told him he wanted to leave the Red Army. The man laughed in his face, and suggested that he wait to see if the poor farmers wouldn't be converted in a couple of days' time. It was only in the hope that they *wouldn't* be that Nikolai Brandeis stayed.

He stayed – and the commissar was proved right. There was no more talk of 'others' property'. Suddenly everything was stood on its head. The rich farmers grovelled, and the poorer ones grew assertive. Parsons in neighbouring villages preached the virtues of redistribution in their sermons. Far from setting Brandeis' mind at rest, these changes confused him utterly. One night he lost his reason. He became obsessed with the idea that the edge of the world must be nearby, from which one would plunge into an abyss of everlasting night. He had a clear vision of the earth as a disc supported on a stalk, something like a mushroom with a frayed edge. He had to reach that edge. He got on a horse and rode south. Somehow – he was unable later to recall those days – he reached the sea. He got as far as Constantinople, and only there did he recover his sanity.

113

But it wasn't his old sanity. It was an entirely different Nikolai Brandeis who now, with a systematic fervour, begged on people's doorsteps and in the streets, who stole the identity papers of a drunken neighbour in an overcrowded little hotel where they slept ten to a room, and then, in the guise of a dumb Macedonian and without understanding a word of Greek or Bulgarian, got on a boat and made the crossing as a ship's fireman, then, as a stowaway and after many adventures, crossed the Balkans, Hungary and Austria to reach Germany, with the support of various aid committees to whom he identified himself variously as a merchant, a colonel, even a general, as the fancy took him. This was a new Nikolai Brandeis. 'How many are you? Are you *one*?' he would ask. 'I'm ten people! I was a teacher, student, farmer, Tsarist, murderer and traitor. I've known peace and plenty, poverty, war, typhoid, starvation, night and day, frost and sweltering heat, danger and life. And all that before I was born! Because today's Nikolai Brandeis was born just two weeks ago.'

He was then thirty-seven years old. He gave himself a limit of five years. By the time those five years were up, he wanted to be a free man. With the implacable rigour that had been a characteristic of his since the time of his madness, he reflected:

'All right, I'm an infant, just embarked on life. What am I doing in this world? Is it worth experiencing? The only freedom I have at the moment is to leave it again. But it appears that the world has a certain attractiveness. It makes me curious. Now, it can hardly provide me with more experiences than I've had already. But there are worse things than to have all my experience under my belt, and to look on as others try to gain theirs. People strike me as peculiar because in each of them I can find a piece of the old, dead Nikolai Brandeis. They still have ideals and principles, schools and houses, identities and passports. They are patriotic and unpatriotic, sabre-rattlers and pacifists, nationalists and internationalists. I am none of those things. I had countries, fatherlands in the past, but they went under. I believed in things, they evaporated. The death of a single parson made it all clear to me. I find it strange that people don't believe in miracles. They're prepared to believe in anything else, but not in miracles. I have experienced miracles. Now, who, among all those believers in ideas, who ever experienced their idea like that?

'This style of observing and reflecting pleases me. If I were to say that that's the purpose of my life, then I would consider that enough to justify staying in this world, now that I have entered it. In order to enjoy my independence, I need freedom. The way the world is constituted today – and it interests me, which is almost as much as to say I like it – you need money to be free. So I have two alternatives: either die or get rich. Now it's perfectly possible to die a rich man, but a dead man can't get rich. So, it's money!'

Such a line of reasoning surely never made a rich man of anyone, but Nikolai Brandeis was an exception. It was this reasoning – and nothing else – that marked the beginning of his wealth. Who knows what governs chance? Perhaps it was that reasoning of Brandeis' that created the chance which brought him money.

That chance was a perfectly mundane operation, and it's only for the sake of completeness that it's set down here:

In Danzig Brandeis met a Russian émigré who had lost all his money at the casino in Soppot, and was just about to sell his wife's diamond necklace. He asked Brandeis to find him a buyer for it, but Brandeis urged him to try one last time.

'Sell the necklace,' he said. 'Give me half the money. Then I'll go and play for you in Soppot. If I lose, I owe you the money, and even though I've got nothing today, I'll do everything I can to pay you back. And if I win, then I get 10 per cent of your winnings.'

When he went to the tables he knew he would win. It was only a fit of superstition that had made him ask for just 10 per cent. He played and won. When he had won three times in a row, he got up and left. The 10 per cent he had earned was his first capital.

His unshakeable indifference guaranteed his success. Yes, it sometimes seemed as though the unpredictable whims of his imagination could intuit the unpredictable course that money likes to take. To the others it was unfathomable. He himself thought it only to be expected that a man like himself, without any commitments and determined since his birth – as he called his desertion – to make money, should be able to do so. He was proof that what one needs to become rich isn't cool calculation, but inspiration. He followed every inspiration he had.

By now three of the five years were up. He was starting to grow wealthy. For a few weeks he had been supplying the police forces of a couple of Balkan states with cloth.

10

The noonday bells died away. The hobnailed column disappeared in a small cloud of dust and noise. The street was left deserted. People were eating in their homes and in restaurants. The spring breeze carried the aromas of Sunday lunch.

Nikolai Brandeis sat down at a café terrace. Two men walked by, and his ear picked up the sound of Russian. Brandeis hadn't cared to share his predicament with anyone. He avoided occasions that forced him to listen – with a show of credulity – to the émigrés' tales of their past glories, and to overlook – with a show of blindness – whatever of their present misery they revealed in spite of themselves. For who among them had been reborn by their flight, the way he had been? They all seemed to have left their lives behind in Russia. The balalaika strummings of their nostalgia bored him every bit as much as the marching tunes that he had just heard. Though a deserter himself, he couldn't understand the kind of patriotism that bewails a thoroughly extant fatherland as though it had been wiped off the face of the earth. Those people were really crying for their silver samovars.

Nevertheless, the Russian words he had just heard seemed to settle in some unfamiliar part of Brandeis' mind, a part that the spring must have uncovered. They revived his memories of February in the Ukraine, the way a long-awaited rain revives parched fields. Memories blossomed in him. He could clearly distinguish all the subtle nuances and gradations of spring in his homeland. He remembered days in February when for five minutes at noon the sun was able to generate a comforting warmth, enough to make the icicles on the roofs suddenly start to drip, and it was as though the sun had just performed a short practice routine for the summer ahead. The blue of the sky was still a wintry cobalt. Only round the edges was it a lighter colour, almost white, as if it had iced over there. And yet the air felt warm and moist, as if in anticipation of summer rain. Already – invisible to the human eye – it contained the stuff of summer clouds. Then the northeast wind would sweep down, and instantly the icicles refroze. Night would fall in the village faster than on previous days, even though they had surely been shorter. In the gloaming, only the silver birches in the little wood opposite would shimmer, standing in amongst the other trees like slips of days amongst ancient nights. In the fields, little reddish bonfires awoke, on which potatoes were roasted. The sweet smell of the burning twigs wafted into the village. Today you would still be able to walk across the wide swamp without having to stick to the safe paths that were marked out by familiar willows. It would still be frozen hard, and ice would splinter like glass under your heel. But how many more times would you be able to walk carefree over the swamp like that? Not more than twenty! Then the blue will-o'-the-wisps would appear like terrestrial stars.

118

Tomorrow, when the moon started to wane, there might be as much snow as back in early November. There would be a heavy snowfall, but you knew it would all be gone in two or three weeks. That, thought Brandeis, was the way things would be looking there today. And I'm sitting here, where spring's only heralds are those denatured city trees, those fools marching, and the smell of roast lamb in the kitchens. What am I doing here?

It was as though the Russian sounds he had heard were a part of the spring in his memory, as though Russian wasn't a means of communication for a certain group of people, but rather the language that nature spoke in that part of the world, the language of the birches and willows, the swamps, the icicles, the wind and the sun and the bonfires. Why those émigrés again? Who knows, perhaps today they all had the same memories he did. That's why it felt good to hear Russian spoken on a day like today. He paid and left.

He walked without paying attention to where he was going. He wanted to go to a restaurant, not because he was hungry, more out of a kind of sense of obligation, in compliance with the instruction that the whole eating city imparts to the individual, the tacit suggestion of lunch. He realised that his recollections could be called by no other name than homesickness. It was his first experience of it. He gave a start. What was happening to him? Was there yet another Nikolai Brandeis coming into being?

All unawares, he had got as far as Marburger Strasse. His homesickness had communicated itself first of all to his feet, the instruments of migration. They had found their own way. And he was standing in front of the

119

Russian restaurant where he had gone to eat that first month after his arrrival, and never since. They had changed the decor, there was a new management now, and the waiters wore stiff collars, there was a cigarette girl in a blue pageboy uniform, and the cloakroom tokens were of brass. He glanced at the snacks laid out on the table in the middle of the room. They had lost the authenticity they had had in the old, impoverished days. Already they resembled compromises that had been reached with Berlin traditions. They were submitting to change, like all emigrants. The vodka he ordered was ridiculously mild. He said as much to the waiter, in Russian, with an expression of offended pride. He was brought a different one.

Two men at the next table stopped their conversation and looked at him eagerly, as one looks at a fellow-unfortunate. He greeted them. They seemed pleasant enough. Both were bald, and you could see the reflection of the lights on their skulls. But otherwise they were as different from each other as only Russians can be, belonging to a vast nation that consists of a great many small ones. In his current mild disposition he had nothing against émigrés. That little dark one with the yellowish complexion and black moustache came from the southern Ukraine. The tall fair one, with the long head, no eyebrows and pinkish colouring that blushes easily, must be from Poland or one of the Baltic republics. And yet both of them are first-class Russians. They share the same tastes, the same type of digestion, their bodies respond to alcohol in the same way. The same as mine, a German Jew. What we all have in common is the type of our

120

physical needs. Nikolai Brandeis raised a glass to his neighbours.

He listened to their conversation. They were talking about one Joseph Danilovitch, who was apparently waiting for an even more profitable wave of inflation to hit Paris. Suddenly it seemed vital to the taciturn Brandeis to warn his neighbours, and through them the completely unknown Joseph Danilovitch. He joined in their conversation. They were glad to listen to what he had to say.

'There is only one long-term consequence of the French inflation: the lower value of the franc on the gold standard. Unlike Germany, France doesn't have too many banknotes circulating. Also the Banque de France has enough gold, 3654 million, which is equivalent to about 60 per cent of the money in circulation. The Frenchman in the street has confidence in the currency, which is a factor of crucial importance in its stabilisation. Either the debt will be consolidated, or they will debit their capital, or, I think the likeliest outcome, they will take out a foreign loan, using the Banque de France's gold as a guarantee.

'Of course the Banque de France could also decide to draw on their gold reserves directly, and by my calculations that would still mean 2500 million left to back the currency. The English won't press France too hard, they'll be pliant. France will stop believing that there are fortunes to be squeezed out of Germany. So in fact they're almost out of the woods already.'

It was a pleasure for him to put them right. They listened, realising that here was an expert, a man who followed the movements of the stock exchange from the lofty perspective of a statesman. 'We want to go to Paris ourselves, but for other reasons, nothing to do with business.'

'Well,' said Brandeis, 'in that case I suggest you take plenty of money with you.'

He rose. They asked him for his address. For a moment he regretted having become involved with them, but he told them his address.

He wanted to take a long, roundabout way home. The word 'home' made him smile. He had been living in the hotel for two years now. Suddenly it struck him as impossible to go on staying there. Sundays were insufferable there, Sunday afternoons in particular. The sound of love and gramophones leaked out of all the rooms. The landlady, a court councillor's widow, would wear her black-and-grey silk. On top of the wardrobe in Nikolai's room was a violin case with the court councillor's old instrument in it. 'We always used to have quartets in these rooms,' the widow would say. Brandeis pictured the blue and white of his limewashed room. In his nostrils he still had the scent of hay, dung, the mustiness of the hen-roost, the trenchant odour of the cowshed, the hot, hissing stream of horse-piss. And then he remembered the hotel's own blend of boiled fish and carbolic soap. He decided not to return till after nightfall.

It came sooner than he'd expected. There, that was Sunday over. Sunday evenings were actually worse outside than they were 'at home'. He fled.

There were two gentlemen waiting for him in the 'salon'. He went in there. They were the two Russians he'd talked to in the restaurant.

122

It turned out they were both chronically shy. They did things together – by the peculiar rule that pairs off the same weakness with itself, sends two plain girls out walking together, embroils two deaf people in a conversation, and induces two shy people to team up in the hope that together they will be bold. The fair one, who was younger than his dark friend, was finally forced to break the awkward silence. He began:

'We're both very glad we happened to meet you. We need your advice. The Joseph Danilovitch we were talking about earlier has put us in an unpleasant situation. That's why we've come to you, because we assumed you'd be interested in art.'

'Me? In art?' said Brandeis. 'Never!'

His visitors looked so crestfallen at this that he felt obliged to add: 'But perhaps that needn't prevent me from giving you an opinion. What kind of art are we talking about? Painting?'

'No,' replied the other, 'theatre. We have a cabaret you may have heard of. It was founded five years ago. We've performed all over the place, had good nights and bad, but we always managed to keep going, with the help of that Joseph Danilovitch we mentioned. As long as he was able to stay in the black. Since the stabilisation of the currency, we haven't had a squeak out of him. He hasn't replied to letters or telegrams. Right now, our company's in Belgrade. It's almost the end of our run there. Next week we have an engagement in Paris. But the box office has been poor in Belgrade. Think of the competition! They've got the Bluebird, the Golden Cock, the Balalaika and the White Cottage. We're fifth in line. And we're

123

good. Only the public there is spoilt for choice. We won't have any money for the trainfare to Paris.'

'What's your company called?'

'The Green Swan,' they both announced at once, like officers naming their regiment.

Nikolai Brandeis could vaguely remember seeing posters with that name on them. In the polite frame of mind he was in today, he remarked that he had heard a lot of good things about their work.

Then would he be able to help them? they both asked.

'It so happens I've got some business in Belgrade, and I'll drop in on you while I'm there.'

The men left.

11

Now he was in Belgrade.

In the afternoon he watched the rehearsals at the Green Swan.

He couldn't remember when he had last gone to the theatre. Two or three years ago perhaps. He'd gone several times, with the kind of expectancy he remembered having felt years previously, as a student. He'd gone, and had seen empty stages – even when there were actors moving about on them. That, he thought, must be the intention of modern theatre directors – the emptiness of the stage must have dawned on some theatre people at least. That's why so many sets had staircases. When he saw a staircase, he had the impression of sitting in front of a gutted house. He remembered seeing the effects of an earthquake in the Caucasus. In a few streets at the edge of the small old town the walls and roofs of the houses had collapsed, and you could see inside them, planks, beams, and a staircase going nowhere. The sky arched overhead, and the staircase, which must once have led up to the top of the house, now seemed so ridiculously small, in view of the infinite distance between the top step and the lowest cloud that, for all that it had stayed intact, it showed the magnitude of the disaster more clearly than all the rubble and destruction.

Brandeis had been the more appalled at the spectacle offered by these stages because the image of destruction that they presented was not caused by any catastrophe, but by a human agency called 'direction'. Sometimes he was curious to meet one of these 'directors'. What catastrophes there must be in the minds of such men, what nightmares must haunt them. Because all too clearly what they put on stage were the hollow abysses into which their dreams plunged them at night. There had still been limelight in Brandeis' youth. Now, when he returned to the theatre, there were spotlights – not so much illuminating the hollow night of the stage as drilling through it. All the same, it was never dark enough to make the spectator forget that this darkness had been constructed: out of the shadows of the junk and crates and the hanging lofts whose preserved, mummified death cast a kind of mechanical chill over the mimed action. And although the spotlight set the actors in little holes of light, it still wasn't bright enough to make the spectators forget the private reality of the actor. Rather, it was as though the spotlight represented the spectator's curiosity – the only curiosity the spectator might still feel at a modern production – a curiosity whose subject was not the meaning of the action, but rather the meaninglessness of the movements. It was as though the spotlight's tenacious pursuit of the actor was motivated by its puzzlement at why the man who had just climbed three stairs to speak a sentence had to go down them again to hear the reply. It seemed to Brandeis that less had been asked of the theatre in his youth, and so it had been able to give more. He was quite sure that he had not gone to the theatre to see Shakespeare, as they say, 'brought to life' – because Shakespeare could never be more alive than when one read him – but rather to see the difference between the Shakespeare that was performed on stage and the one who lived in the spectator's own imagination. From time to time it happened that a great actor – just because neither he nor the stage (proscenium arch, wings, cardboard trees and rocks and walls) ever denied for one instant that they were theatre – had absorbed a poetic destiny in his body, and offered his own blood for the blood of Shakespeare. But today's director, thought Brandeis, would direct the actor in his self-sacrifice, which, to win grace, had to take place in complete solitude. Direction creates space. Now there was no one to fill it, therefore the space was left dark, in the hope that the slender cone of light would rescue the human being. What an error! The human being was tied to a hole, and, trapped in the hollowness his own body had become, he stumbled through the night.

Brandeis would never have talked to anyone about all that. He didn't think it was his business. He didn't claim to know anything about it. It wasn't 'his thing'. It horrified him to think that in the modern theatre they went around shouting the way they did in the stock exchange. He thought it a shabby thing to pay for a fiction that didn't admit it was one. For a play that purported to contain a heightened version of life, but, compared to Brandeis' own adventures from his previous existence, or even to his recent supplying of material to the Balkans, was anything but heightened life, rather it was the pale reflection of some bloodless dramatist's dream of what life was. No! He preferred the cinema. He loved the innocent darkness of the auditorium, and the illuminated shadows of the protagonists. He loved the primitive excitement of the fiction, which owned up to what it was. He loved the isolation in which each person sat, because everyone seemed to be pressed up against the screen. They left their bodies – like coats in a cloakroom – on the seats. Brandeis went to the cinema twice a week. It relaxed him. He didn't speak. He didn't hear anything. He sat impatiently through the short intervals when they changed the reels, which he hated. He thought some day he would start a chain of cinemas where the lights never came up.

He went to the rehearsals of the Green Swan, and sat alone in the dark auditorium. It proved to him once more that he wasn't interested in art, still less in theatricals. In fact the Russian cabaret, familiar to him from before the Revolution, was something he'd always detested. He disliked a form that, for fear of scale, turns coy. He hated cuteness. He hated the sketches where people turned into Lilliputians, farmers' wives into ballerinas, and Cossacks into toy soldiers. He hated the vapid charm of the emcee, who told a special joke in his honour – already he was being treated like an 'angel'. Why didn't he get out? Now he was watching the rehearsals for the third time. Yes, and he even looked in at the theatre at night to hear what the box office had been like. Why did he do it?

The company was in trouble. They hadn't paid their hotel bills for some time. They were no longer permitted to eat on tick. There were some nights when they made just enough to buy a bun each and a cup of tea or coffee in a café. After every performance they would sit huddled together round tables, like groups of clucking chickens waiting for the butcher's knife. And yet they remained boisterous, because they were afraid of silence, as if silence inevitably meant death. In all the years of their existence they had never known such a bad time. Their hurriedly wiped-down faces had a sickly yellow gleam in the evening lights. And yet they wouldn't leave each other's company. Every night they sat there till closing time. And after that they would drift about between the three hotels where they were put up. All of them. And the little clutch that finally disappeared into their own hotel felt wretched and betrayed by the others. They would stand around in the corridors whispering. When finally the door closed behind each of them, it sounded like a coffin lid.

Brandeis asked them one evening: 'Why don't you all go your separate ways?'

They looked at him aghast and a little askance, as though they thought he was mad, and a little inferior as well. 'What?' replied the bandleader, 'and break up the Green Swan? Never!' And Brandeis realised that these people had raised a feeling of community to an artistic principle. They hadn't always been actors. The women came from good homes, some of the men had been officers and civil servants, there were a couple of landowners among the musicians, and the bandleader had been a schoolmaster.

For Brandeis it was his first chance to spend money on something he didn't care for. Ever since going into business, he had seen every item of expenditure as an investment of some sort. Giving money to a beggar would have seemed as nonsensical to him as lighting a fire just to extinguish it a moment later, or as dropping his watch on the pavement to make it stop ticking. He had given two thousand dollars to Theodor Bernheim because he had wanted Paul's help, and also because it was a principle with him to impede, wherever possible, the functioning of earthly justice. He would have liked to help every one of the multitude of Theodors to get clear of the police. He hated the institution of the state. He couldn't understand it. But still less could he understand the art and theatre that flourished in the ornamental gardens of the reviled institution.

And yet he paid the Green Swan's hotel bills and their train fares to Paris.

It was their last night in Belgrade. They were sitting in little groups at various tables in their regular café, noisy and exultant at the prospect of going to Paris. Brandeis entered. He was returning to Berlin that night, and was looking for the manager to say goodbye. He felt ridiculous. He had spent money on a ridiculous enterprise, he had had a pointless journey, and just wasted his time. Now he wanted to put all that behind him. In fact, he thought, it would have been better to leave without seeing them again. But that's what you do when you've been given money, not when you're giving it.

They spotted him the moment he stepped into the café, they clustered round him, and treated him with profuse gratitude – as was only proper. He looked indifferently round at their indifferent faces. Suddenly his eye was drawn to an empty space.

There was one face missing. He didn't know the name of it. He missed it, nothing more.

He sat down at a table and ordered a drink. A moment ago he had been proposing to leave as quickly as possible, without delay. And now he was sitting down to wait. The face he was waiting for couldn't be more than nineteen years old. The longer the space remained unfilled, the more clearly he could see it: the hollow cheeks, the wide, red, painted mouth, like a scream in the calm face, and the dark eyes so close together that the eyebrows seemed to join up. What shoes is she wearing? Suddenly that was the vital question. He would have liked to ask what shoes she was wearing, even though he'd never asked after her at all previously. He didn't even know her name. Of course I could describe her. But that would be embarrassing. I'd rather wait. I'll go to Berlin tomorrow.

His train was leaving at eleven. When she appeared, it was just ten by the big clock over the buffet. He only had an hour. He thought it was cruel of her to time her arrival like that, and tempt him to travel tonight, when he'd all but given that up. Why now? Half an hour wasn't enough to learn everything about her that he might need to know. But to say goodbye to her half an hour was ample. Was there anything else he'd had in mind? So far as he could remember, that was his sole purpose in staying. She'd arrived, and now he could take his leave of her. But it might have been better if her appearance had coincided with the departure of the train. Then there would be three hours till the café closed. After that there were other places one might go. And the train to Paris that the Green

Swan were taking, that didn't leave till 3 o'clock tomorrow afternoon. An absurd hope struck Brandeis: what if the clock over the buffet was slow? It was simple, he just needed to take his watch out of his waistcoat pocket. But he put off doing so, because he was afraid of seeing that the clock had been right all along. Finally he took out his watch. It was as though he'd emerged from a bitter frost into bright sunshine: it was way past eleven. His train was already off and running.

'What's the name of the woman who's just come in?' he asked a neighbour.

'That's Lydia. Lydia Markovna.'

'Lydia Markovna,' Brandeis repeated. He stood up and walked towards her. She had come in slowly, all smiles. Now, as she approached her friends, she was deciding which table to sit at. Nikolai Brandeis stood right in front of her, so close that she had to tilt her head back to look him in the face. She held out her hand. He pulled her over to an empty table.

'You're Lydia Markovna,' he said, as though to confirm it was really her, as though no other name would do.

'Yes – haven't you seen me before?'

'Yes, I've seen you. But I don't ask after names. Only in very special cases. Yours, for example, is a very special case.'

He waited. She said simply: 'Why?'

'Because I'd like you – ' Brandeis said, 'because I'd like to ask you not to leave with the others tomorrow, but to go home with me.'

'What? And leave the theatre?'

'Why not?'

'But – you've no idea. I have a boyfriend. I can't leave him. I don't know you!'

'Which one's your boyfriend?'

'Grigori – that's him over there.'

Brandeis looked round. He was the man with the bass voice who played the First Cossack in the White Cavalry sketch.

Grigori was involved in a game of cards.

'Wait here,' said Nikolai.

He sent the waiter across to Grigori with a piece of paper on which he'd written:

'Come right away. It's about money.'

Grigori came. He looked alternately at Lydia, whom he didn't greet, and at Brandeis, whom he simply beamed at. 'Listen,' said Brandeis quietly, 'is it all right if Lydia Markovna stays behind tomorrow? With me?'

'My dear chap, why are you bothering me?' replied Grigori. 'I thought it was to do with money!'

'You'll get the money. Answer me.'

Grigori narrowed his eyes and looked at Lydia.

Then he said: 'Of course – if she wants to.'

'Grisha!' screamed Lydia, so loud that everyone turned their heads to look. She laid her head on the tabletop and cried, with her forehead pressing against the marble as if she had no more trust in anything except stone and dead things.

'Come,' said Brandeis. He picked her up out of her chair. The manager came over. Brandeis said: 'Lydia Markovna is leaving you. Pay Mr Grigori two months' wages on my account. Goodnight.'

It was another Nikolai Brandeis who stepped out on to the street, with the woman on his arm.

He went with her to where the cars were parked.

12

There is really nothing more to be said of Paul Bernheim, except that he had remained exactly the same.

He was 'pruning' his workforce, a process inseparable from the 'economic growth' in Germany.

Paul Bernheim pruned away. He dismissed both his typists, and finally his private secretary too. He gave up the office over his flat, and then the flat itself. He couldn't conceivably stay on as an ordinary lodger in a building where he'd previously been a lodger *extraordinaire*. He shed various habits: they dropped from him like autumn leaves. The mysterious mechanism that had drawn the proprietor of a barber's shop, armed with brush, soap and razor, up to Paul's room every day at one o'clock in the afternoon, now, just as mysteriously, ceased to function. The rule by which the porter would identify Paul Bernheim's footfall two storeys up, and have the front door open by the time he reached it, was now suspended. One day Paul Bernheim sold his car and dismissed his chauffeur. The car was bought by a taxi firm. Henceforth, thought Paul Bernheim, he would never be able to take a taxi, for fear of climbing into his own car. He dismissed the chauffeur with a gratuity that was far more than he could afford – a kind of desperate *noblesse oblige.* His friends all disappeared, as though some cataclysm had taken them off. He could go through the gaming clubs one after another, they were simply nowhere to be found.

His loneliness stabilised like the currency. He rented a single room, in the delusory hope that his loneliness would thereby decrease, but discovered that it is a characteristic of loneliness actually to be greater in one room than in three. He had miscalculated, as his mother had. She had a suitcase full of banknotes, and he owned shares that didn't provide him with any income. Why hadn't he come in on the cloth deal with Brandeis? He would have been a rich man today. He had come so close. Now he had just two thousand dollars. The two thousand dollars he owed Brandeis. With that, you could just about buy a corner shop. The only profession he might have enjoyed was diplomacy. He could always take out another loan on the house. But as there were already three mortgages on that part of it that had been left to him, he would need his mother's agreement for a further loan. And that was out of the question. Bernheim & Co. was about to go into liquidation anyway. Only his mother didn't know it.

Sometimes Paul Bernheim would calculate his assets, though he knew well enough what they came to. But he thought he might have made a mistake somewhere, and that, by some miracle, totting them up again might produce a different result. If he sold his stock at today's prices, and including the two thousand dollars, he had barely more than twenty-five thousand marks. With that for his starting capital someone else, a Nikolai Brandeis,

136

would have been able to make a million within a couple of years. But Paul Bernheim was one of those people with such grand notions that a small sum of money isn't even fit to be spent.

The spring days were fine, the sky had been given a new coat of blue paint, the road had been scrupulously spring-cleaned, and clouds seemed to have been banished completely. If only I had a car! thought Paul. He couldn't remember there ever being such gorgeous weather when he'd still had one. He felt sullied when he got on a bus or the underground. He was still sleeping on into the afternoon, out of obstinacy and the vague hope that good fortune might accumulate over his sleeping head like a cloud – even though common sense told him to get up early in the morning. Once he was actually up and dressed and on the street, the day itself, nearing its end, seemed to confirm the futility of any effort.

A few times he decided to pay morning calls. He went to the directors of great publishing houses. He had proposals to make. He came prepared to exaggerate his fortune, to speak of credit facilities, and of contacts in England in which he ended up believing himself. He went to one big firm after another. He sat in the waiting rooms, where the publisher's own newspapers and magazines were provided free of charge, to acquaint the visitor with the firm's orientation without anyone being required to tell him what it was. The waiting rooms were comfortable, slightly overheated, and invigilated by liveried commissionaires sitting on tall stools. The directors would invariably be attending meetings. They were no longer the 'important' meetings that Paul had fabricated for himself during the Inflation, they were ordinary meetings, without any particular quality, and actually all the more important for it – in the manner of a great man who has a title, but doesn't use it. He sat and waited, as others had once waited for him. He realised now that the waiting room was the purgatory to capitalism's heaven. No worse torment than to be compelled to patience, perpetually interrupted by bells ringing for messenger-boys, by the arrival of other visitors, by distractedly flicking through magazines intended to give comfort, but in fact productive of the deepest despondency in their readers. Sometimes Bernheim would leave the waiting room without paying his call. And to have avoided a meeting which had lost its point before it could even take place gave him a feeling of liberation, as if he'd been let out of a lunatic asylum. When he left the building's portals he would look behind him, like a man looking back at an obstacle that had made him stumble.

That's the last time I'm ever going in there!

He went to see his mother again.

The Defence Ministry widow was by now so thoroughly settled in, it was as though she'd been born in the Bernheims' house. She greeted Paul like a nephew. Frau Bernheim was still in the habit of prowling around after her lodger, checking if a light hadn't been left on, if there wasn't a wardrobe key dangling so loosely in the lock that it might fall and be lost, if there wasn't a window left open at night, an invitation to passing moths to gorge themselves on the carpet, or if the basin in the widow's room hadn't finally sprung the crack that Frau Bernheim had been expecting for years with trepidation.

'We're agreed now,' she told Paul, 'that Frau Hammer is to take over the subscription to the paper. Just a month ago it rained and some water got into her room, the roof leaked. She said I had to repair it. But I explained to her that a landlady can't be made responsible every time there's a leak in the roof. And she accepted that. The roof was repaired, but we haven't had any rain since then, and I wonder if the builder hasn't cheated us. Would you mind going up and taking a look?'

Paul went up to take a look.

He looked down on the garden, which in spring was an even more dispiriting sight than it had been in the autumn – as a tramp looks more wretched in the sunshine than he does in the fog and rain. Paul saw the empty outbuildings with no cars or carriages in them, the stables where the neighbours' horses could be heard whinnying, and the old dog lying slothfully in the dirt in front of his kennel, as though he knew there was nothing left to guard except the suitcase with Frau Bernheim's useless paper money.

One night, his mother laid aside the newspaper – since her lodger had taken on the payment of the subscription, Frau Bernheim no longer felt obliged to read all the small ads – and said abruptly:

'You know, Paul, the newspaper seems to be full of betrothals!'

'Yes,' said Paul indifferently. 'It's because the war's over.'

'The young people are sensible,' Frau Bernheim went on. 'They marry quickly, which is healthy and guarantees a long life.'

She waited for a reply from her son.

But Paul appeared to be lost in thought. He heard the tick of the clock, the only one that was still going, and last year's cut foliage rustling in the light wind. Frau Bernheim took up her lorgnon, and only the sound of it snapping open recalled Paul to the present.

Frau Bernheim examined Paul through her lorgnon for some minutes. He knew this meant that his mother was preparing to broach a 'serious subject', and he waited.

'You're thirty now, Paul,' said Frau Bernheim.

The reference to his age hurt him, as if it were a physical infirmity. There they were, truly, his thirty years, and what had he done in them? It was as though those three decades, all the years, the months and the days lay piled up beside him, a mountain of time, and he himself was standing next to it, small, passive and ageless.

'Haven't you ever thought of marrying?' his mother asked, a little severely, still looking at him through her lorgnon.

'Where do I find a wife?'

'Oh, there are plenty of women, boy – look around a bit!'

She took off her lorgnon again, and, as though sheathing a sword, let it glide back down to her hips.

There was no more talk of marriage. All the same, returning to Berlin on the train, Paul thought about his mother's suggestion. Yes, perhaps it was time to get married. It was pretty easy to get married. Caution and a quick decision were the important factors. Marriage might lead to greatness. He would start going out again.

From an earlier time, the time when he'd been a sort of patron, he had known a young man named Sandor Tekely from Temesvar, who said he was from Budapest. He had come to Berlin as a draughtsman and journalist, but he might as well have come as a riding tutor, a master of the black arts and a secret agent: fate, which watches over young people from Temesvar with a certain affection, first directed Sandor Tekely to the gaming clubs, then the cabarets, then the theatre, and after a couple of years to the cinema, and only then back to the newspapers. He had once been a member of the PR section accompanying the Red Army of the Hungarian dictator Béla Kun on his campaign against the Romanians. But he had long since forgotten those days and their doings. He was capable of forgetting murder, typhoid and years in jail. This quality in him corresponded to another: his ability to exploit the present. It was as though there was a connection between his forgetfulness and his eye for the main chance, just as there is a connection between the way a robust constitution adapts to winter frosts and summer heatwaves and its ability to shake off illness quickly and thoroughly. It would be unfair to say that Sandor Tekely was 'spineless'. He was forgetful – but he could also be attentive. Just as a butterfly draws nectar from any flower, so Sandor Tekely was able to extract relationships, connections and friendships from any gathering he attended. He was an outstanding example of the changes taking place in society, of the insecurity of the old established classes and their new members, the fluidity of social values and of the terminal perplexity of modern houses which are built with 'reception rooms'.

141

Blithely, and only out for connections, Tekely fluttered from one hostess to another, making no distinction between them, attended fancy dress balls – which in that year went on long after Carnival was over – always in the garb of a rococo princeling, and ordinary soirées in a dinner jacket, with a waistcoat with lapels, and always with a smile, composed of full carmine lips and dazzling even teeth, always prepared to say something amiable at a first meeting, and something intimate at a second.

Not unnaturally, Sandor Tekely now came to Paul Bernheim's mind. Bernheim knew that Tekely was in the habit of eating at a Hungarian restaurant twice a week, so as not to lose contact with his native soil. He went to see him there. Tekely was pleased. He liked being called on by well-dressed men in this restaurant, where for a long time he had eaten on credit. The setting even accentuated his customary warmth, mingling it with a pleasure that communicated the extraordinary importance he attached to the visit and the man making it.

Where had Paul Bernheim, 'my dear, dear friend', been all this time?

And himself?

Oh, he had nothing to hide! Occupations too numerous to mention. First he was an executive in the advertising company that had been responsible for devising the latest medium, on the postmarks on the top of newspapers. Then he was involved in the PR department of the big American film company that had been in Germany for six months now. Thirdly, with a friend, he was organising a newsletter appearing in all the European languages, carrying news and cultural items.

Fourthly, he was looking after the translation rights of German authors abroad, and foreign authors in Germany. Finally, he was coming up with ideas for new comedies and marketing them to famous dramatists. There was something else in the offing, too, something that a man by the name of Nikolai Brandeis was planning.

'What? – Brandeis the Russian?' asked Paul.

'You know him then?' cried Tekely, grabbing Bernheim by the arm. 'You know him personally?'

'Yes,' said Paul. 'What's so odd about that?'

'Oh, nothing odd, but it's a magnificent contact!'

And Tekely's feigned esteem changed into genuine admiration. 'Brandeis, Brandeis – ' he kept crying out, as a runner in classical times might have called out the name of a victory. 'Don't you know? Brandeis is coming up very fast. One of those men from the east who come to Berlin and make their fortune. Six months ago he bought a dozen apartment blocks on the Kurfürstendamm. He's starting to open department and clothing stores all over the country. Apparently he means to flood the country with these stores of his. Every little town's going to have one. They have the slogan: "For the Middle Class". He broadcasts appeals for the salvation of the middle class, he's started up a bank, and he's supposed to have this fabulously wealthy and beautiful wife he met in Serbia. He's old enough to be her father. You see them together at all the premières. They say she's a Russian princess who fled to Belgrade, with incredible jewellery. She was on the point of selling it off when Brandeis ran into her. How long is it since you saw him last? Give him a ring if you know him! Or hold on: maybe he'll be at the "Black and White" tomorrow.'

'What's the "Black and White"?'

'The new hockey club's fancy dress party, don't you know. Like an invite? Here! Got a pen? I'll write your name in. You're Dr Paul Bernheim, yes?'

It was a clear evening, the sky as bright as early morning, and the moon was so close and familiar that it looked like a big brother to the silver streetlamps. Paul blessed Tekely. 'You should meet someone like that at least twice a week. The fellow knows everything, and he brings luck with it. Now everything depends on this "Black and White" do. Either something decisive will happen there, or nothing ever will. "Black and White", here we come. Hockey's a grand game!'

13

The great hall of the Casino, where the party was taking place, had been turned into a labyrinth. Unexpected nooks between mock walls, sitting areas and hideaways had the function not only of offering invisibility to guests wishing to indulge in illicit pleasures, but also of keeping them constantly afraid of being interrupted. For there was no secluded corner that did not also have a hidden access to it. The designer had a sadistic bent.

Paul Bernheim finally chose a position near the entrance, so as to get a view of the new arrivals. Brandeis was not among them. 'I might have guessed,' said Paul. 'That Sandor Tekely has led me up the garden path often enough.' He felt sad and embittered. Everyone at this hockey club bash knew everyone else, disguise or not. Yes, and they had probably all tipped off their friends beforehand. There was so much the feeling of belonging to one family that the few lost-looking strangers – probably all of them there at Tekely's invitation – were viewed like gatecrashers, with surprise and a little resentment. Two dance orchestras faced each other from separate platforms. There was no let-up. The moment a shy silence started to flower after one ensemble had finished a tango, the other would assault the silent minute with a jazz number, and grind it to pieces with its drums and saxophones. Couples danced indefatigably. In this closed, if disguised, company, Paul Bernheim could see no possibility of making any decisive meeting, however fervently he wished for it all evening. He was dressed in a dark domino, a costume he thought lent itself to significant encounters. But none presented itself.

Or shall we say: none seemed to present itself. For a girl in harem costume, with a golden breastplate and a broad turquoise headband, wearing loose white trousers and blue sandals with golden buckles, pulled Paul into a corner, with the gentle violence employed by women who lead law-abiding lives, and which gives the impression that they would like nothing better than to copy the obscene movements of a harbourfront prostitute. It was almost 2 a.m., and Bernheim no longer hoped for anything worthwhile to happen. So he abandoned himself to the undemanding pleasure of holding the girl's body against his own. She asked for a drink, and he got up to bring her a glass of champagne, which they were dishing out at the buffet. He could see that she was trying to heighten the slight thrill she already felt. What was the point of a fancy dress ball, she thought. I'm bored. Everyone recognises me, and no one will so much as try a joke. This young man's a stranger. He may not be any smarter than the others, but at least he's got the advantage of not knowing who I am.

So she simply told him she was bored. She complained about the unadventurous men, whom she referred to by their first names or nicknames. She fired Paul's ambition, and reminded him of the happy years of his first youth, in which – with Oxford beckoning – he had cheerfully seduced the girls of his home town just to the extent that didn't compromise their prospects as future brides. Still, they were pretty chaste times really, he thought to himself. No girl would have been so straightforward with him then, even in fancy dress. His constant impulse, inherited from his mother, to classify strangers by social background – regardless of their sex – led him to conclude from the girl's behaviour that she was not from what he called the 'top drawer'. And as men do who compute a woman's resistance by her father's income, he decided to go as far – or as near – as the remoteness and darkness of the place would permit.

He received a few encouraging rebuffs at first. The breastplate loosened somewhat. His endeavours were already so bold that he had reached the stage of being oblivious to the woman's face and individuality, and was only conscious of her sex. Then a noise startled him. A rococo prince had passed by and spoken his name softly. He asked the girl to wait for him, and set off after the prince. It was Sandor Tekely.

'Congratulations on your conquest!' said Tekely.

'She's not bad-looking, is she?' replied Bernheim. He felt somewhat frosty, both at being interrupted, and because Tekely had placed something rather more important in prospect yesterday.

'Yes, she's pretty,' said Tekely. 'But that's not the main thing. You know who she is, of course?'

'Not a clue!'

147

'No use lying, my friend. You know perfectly well that that's Fräulein Irmgard Enders.'

'Enders Chemicals?'

'Yes. I'd get back in there if I were you.'

Paul Bernheim hurried back.

Fräulein Enders was waiting for him. But she was baffled by the change that seemed to have come over her man. Because now that Paul knew the identity of his partner, he found it impossible to move a muscle. And whereas previously he'd been entirely indifferent to her face, now he felt he must see it.

'Oh, you've gone all boring,' remarked Fräulein Enders, with some reason. And she made a move to get up.

He held her down forcibly, blessing Sandor Tekely once more. And then he started to talk. If his hands were paralysed, at least he could still move his tongue. He felt that his life depended on this girl, and that he must avoid boring her at all costs. With that reverence for the chemical industry which in men of Paul Bernheim's type conditions all their values and standards and exhausts their capacity for admiration and respect; with that reverence for chemistry itself, magical as its formulae, great as the faith of the believer, the loyalty of true monarchists to kings and emperors, and the reverence of some peoples for the dead: with that reverence Paul Bernheim now began to watch Fräulein Enders, to entertain and to court her. The spectre of failure was forever in front of him. He was unable to recover his former temerity. He tried. Fräulein Enders had liked it. Now he oscillated anxiously between his fear of offending the majesty of chemistry, which he carried deep in his heart, and his desire to hold it in so little regard that he might be able to take the liberties necessary with the daughters of great men.

He plunged into telling stories, as was his wont (he had the novelist's gift of telling lies), mixing his own experiences and others', borrowed jokes and anecdotes and original ones, to such effect that a quarter of an hour later the old Paul Bernheim had been reborn – the charmer, the dilettante, and the art historian. His eyes' fluttering blue – which the Inflation wheeling and dealing seemed to have slightly dimmed – was now once more so lustrous that Fräulein Enders surely noticed it, in spite of the subdued lighting. He pointed his stories in such a way that, if they didn't pierce the heart of the girl like Cupid's arrows, they would at least fire her imagination. And he was so good at casually being the hero of his own tales, that even his bragging had the appearance of modesty. He was in full flight. He didn't forget to intersperse tales of his courage with others that showed his trembling humanity, so that Fräulein Enders, struck by his qualities as a man of action, was also impressed by his frankness. She enjoyed herself in Paul's company. As she gathered from his stories that he had been to Oxford, she naturally assumed that he was related to the English aristocracy – the only one still occasionally capable of impressing our chemical knights. But when she heard that his name was plain Paul Bernheim – for he made a point of telling it to her – then the young man became imbued with mystery, which is even more important to a girl than being aristocratic and English.

149

She was supposed to be giving a close family friend a lift home, but she opted for Paul's company instead. Her car, waiting at the corner, and the chauffeur – generations of service in his profile, which had been sharpened up by artificial means – enchanted Paul as lovers of an earlier age would have been enchanted by a glimpse of garter. And he felt quite beside himself with delight when he saw that there was a corgi in the car, wrapped in a rug, a dog redolent of Oxford and of English lawns. Making a final lung-bursting effort, he managed to overcome his reverence for the girl's class and to find the strength and the presence of mind – just three minutes away from the Hotel Adlon – to put his arm round her. He had remembered just in time that physical contact is still the thing least liable to be forgotten.

And so it proved. Paul Bernheim was the first man to impress Fräulein Irmgard Enders. A couple of tutors who used to interrupt their lessons in the garden on sultry and stimulating summer afternoons – she was eighteen at the time – to make love to her, could hardly count. They were domestic servants whose attentions, abstracted from their persons, had been automatic, like mercenary services. And, apart from them, there were only harmless chums, the tennis and swimming partners, tobogganers at Arosa, and Charleston dancers. But this young Paul Bernheim had seen the world, he must have rich experiences, an interesting job – which she had not got around to ascertaining – know interesting people and good society too, could speak knowledgeably about horses and cars, and he had a nice face – Irmgard thought it was nice, anyway.

She looked at herself in the mirror, in her costume, and liked what she saw. She generally did. Her legs weren't bad. Not bad at all. The ankles were a little thick compared to her calves, but in trousers they looked slender enough. Everything else immaculate. A little high-breasted, but the shoulders sufficiently developed, and white and enticing, that when she was in evening dress the breasts could almost be forgotten. Not a bit of tummy. Hips wide – too much riding, perhaps? Wrists strengthened by tennis, but slender hands and tapering fingers. Her fair face unremarkable, the mouth perhaps a little small for her liking, especially as her teeth were too big. An ominous line under her chin – what was that? She was only twenty-one. Must have come from the awful way she had of lowering her head over her book when reading. Better give reading a miss.

When Uncle Carl came to collect her the day after tomorrow, she would try him out. Perhaps he would have heard of Paul Bernheim. Thank God her parents weren't alive any more. Her friends Lisa, Inge and Hertha didn't have the kind of freedom she did. No cars, chauffeurs, dogs or fancy dress balls for them. But then, they weren't really characters either. While Irmgard – how she detested the name, a pre-war favourite! – she, Irmgard, was a character. She could find a man on her own. She had excellent taste. She could be tough, she disliked sentimentality, and even if her status as a *demi-vierge* bothered her a bit, at least she knew it was more male feebleness that was to blame than any fault of her own.

She went to bed well satisfied, and began dreaming one of the dreams of her generation: an open sports car,

151

silver-grey, and so on. Just as the first houses of a village were approaching, the dream disappeared, and an uninterrupted, dreamless sleep took over, which lasted until eleven o'clock the following morning.

14

Irmgard's uncle, Herr Carl Enders, didn't come on Thursday as expected, but on Sunday instead. When his wife spoke of her concern for Irmgard's safety in Berlin, Herr Enders would say: 'You don't know Irmgard! You don't know the young people of today! You're living in the past!' He worshipped youth, speed, progress, new inventions and sports. He felt at home in this new age, and he kept himself young and healthy in order to live on into an even newer one. If, in the popular science magazines he subscribed to, and which he read with an almost vicious pleasure, as though they were pornography, he saw an article about a total eclipse of the sun that was predicted for Central Europe towards the end of the third millennium, he would feel distraught at not being able to go on living for another thousand years. And really, when one looked at the man, one could see no reason why he shouldn't go on forever. He had engineers and officials, chemists and assistants, factory managers, secretaries and cashiers working for him, although he himself was busy all day too, and loved being busy and talking about it. He was pointlessly industrious. The world's philosophers and poets, its thinkers and inventors and explorers thought for him, and kept his brain supplied with information. It was to please him that aviators flew across oceans, that record-breakers set out on expeditions by bicycle, sledge and kayak, that Arctic explorers perished, that acrobats broke their necks attempting a triple salchow mortale. At the end of every year he would enthusiastically peruse the accident statistics, and hold the pedestrians responsible for their own deaths. To be slow and absent-minded was a crime against the god Velocity. He himself was often unpunctual, and was given to talking superfluous nonsense. He chaired innumerable conferences, travelled from town to town, went to museums, attended concerts of new music, financed the building of new homes and offices, and subsidised the avant-garde theatre. Before the war, he had been an ardent supporter of Kaiser Wilhelm. During the war, he favoured annexation, less out of hard political conviction than because he loved a good disaster. After the collapse, he became a conservative democrat of the kind that exists only in Germany: at once patriotic and internationalist, honoured to be in the company of a prince, and yet with a pitying smile for him, respecting Socialism but thinking it utopian, building workers' estates from which workers were excluded, having close friends who were Jews and holding office in anti-Semitic associations, voting for a conservative party and even being selected as its candidate, and rejoicing at a victory of the left, rejecting Bolshevism and adoring Soviet Russia.

Knowing her uncle as she did, Irmgard should have known that a man of such diverse inclinations and occupations would not come when he was expected. She

154

believed in the importance of his activities, his travels and his love affairs. And whenever he was late, she always blamed it on some unforeseen obstacle. In this she resembled her aunt. When Herr Enders finally arrived on Sunday, he met an Irmgard who was already, in her fashion, in love. She had met Paul Bernheim three times in the intervening days. Once for tea, once for an aimless drive, and the third time – when they'd arranged to play tennis – for a slow and blissful walk. Tomorrow they were going riding.

To demonstrate his connoisseurship of young people, and his ability to detect the slightest symptoms in his niece, Herr Enders observed:

'We're in love, aren't we?'

Irmgard, to whom her uncle appeared just as old-fashioned as he appeared modern to himself, was offended by the expression 'in love'. It was a condition that didn't seem appropriate to a young woman of today.

'In love?' she replied. And, after a pause, 'Let's just say prepared to marry.'

'Well,' said Herr Enders, 'I'm glad you're sufficiently modern not to confuse love and marriage. You realise you can't marry simply anyone. You may fall in love with anyone though, if you like.'

'I can make up my own mind, uncle.'

'Except in that!'

He recalled the many men who had come to ask him for Irmgard's hand. They had been all sorts: mostly artists to whom he had given support, and whom he ruled out straight away because art was connected in his mind with sexual impotence. He failed to realise he was prejudiced, because he was forever proving – merely by repeatedly saying it – that he was free from prejudice. 'I've got nothing against poor people,' he would say. 'God knows I try to deal with the poor exactly as I do with the rich, but that doesn't mean you adopt them into the family. Now, if it was a genius, someone exceptional, an Eckener, an Einstein, even a Lenin for all I care! A somebody!' And since he had met no 'somebodies' among the poor people he knew, his relations with them remained distant.

For a while he had considered pairing Irmgard off with one of the scions of the aristocracy whom he was forever supporting, inviting over, housing and feeding. He helped start up journals that advocated a united Europe, and others that were spoiling for the next war. And he took out subscriptions to them too. But there was one instinct that kept him from tying the knot with any of his poorer friends, that was mightier than his generosity or philanthropy, and that was the instinct to hang on to his money. Irmgard was to marry a man of exceptional wealth. Either someone from an established landowning family, or else a young industrialist. Herr Enders wasn't aware that between the extremes of plutocracy and penury there was a third condition whose members could at least live in comfort. Men who earned less than half a million a year were poor in his book. And when he imagined poverty, as he sometimes did, he saw frightful things: syphilitic children, a tubercular wife, a bare mattress, and the family silver sold off. 'That's how the middle class is living today,' he would say. He included in that bracket the managers of his own factories. In his opinion the proletariat was taken care of. First it had Socialism, secondly it had no requirements, and thirdly it had social security.

'So long as it isn't anyone middle class,' he said to Irmgard. 'You'll never escape from their misery.' He was genuinely concerned. His red neck, his muscular cheeks, his whole bluff solid being was at the service of his concern. Irmgard thought he looked comical when he was worried. She laughed.

She had known her uncle would make trouble, and her liking for him immediately turned to contempt, which extended to his physical attributes. His robust health was unappealing to her, his constant enthusiasm for progress hypocritical. After gazing at him silently for a few seconds, the word 'moneybags' came to her mind.

On the afternoon when she took tea with Paul and her uncle in the hotel lobby she was by turns irritated, tender, spiteful and deceitful. Paul lost her sympathy for whole seconds at a time – just by making himself agreeable to her uncle. If she could only have guessed that for that hour the only thing on Paul's mind was making himself agreeable to her uncle! But then, she didn't know men.

What do two men talk about, if one makes chemical products, and the other has no interest but 'getting on'? Why, about art. Paul Bernheim, as always, shone. One might have thought he was a collector himself. Who would have guessed a week ago that he'd be drinking tea with Carl Enders? It was another world. Why had he given up his apartment? He would have been able to give a little *souper* at home. So much more intimate.

'I take it you're a collector yourself,' said Herr Enders, hoping to discover something about the young man's circumstances.

'My father was,' Paul lied. And his son's been forced to sell, thought Herr Enders. But he actually said something else:

'Did your father die a long time ago?'

'Before the war.'

'In which you served.'

'11th Dragoons,' crowed Paul.

Family fallen on hard times, thought the uncle again. And he said: 'The war and the Inflation ruined a lot of families. Quite a few woke up to find themselves in the middle class. I'm often made aware of the wretched lot of the intelligentsia today.'

'But a lot of other people did well out of them too.'

'Yes, the *nouveaux riches*.' The uncle seemed to speak the words out of the corner of his mouth. To sour Herr Enders' mood, it was enough merely to mention the *nouveaux riches*.

In the way of men whose grandfathers had been *nouveaux riches*, he looked down on anyone who only became rich today. He would refer to his grandfather, the founder of the Enders Chemical dynasty, as 'the man who started off with just his ten fingers'. Men who performed similar feats today Carl Enders would describe as 'the fellows with elbows'. As though elbows were sordid, and fingers aristocratic. In order to get the industrialist's good opinion, Paul now began telling a joke featuring the then popular Raffke, the kind of thing that began: Herr Raffke goes to hear Beethoven's Ninth (or to see *Wallenstein* at the National, or any of the other cultural institutions where the old rich know their way around) . . . Herr Enders, like most healthy men, loved jokes. He would laugh heartily at any joke, and because he had a short memory, he didn't mind hearing the same one ten times.

Irmgard was grumpily silent. In order not to lose her affection for Paul – which had by now become part of her own self-esteem – she changed her poor opinion of his jokes to an admiration of his ability to get on with her uncle.

Herr Enders came away with the suspicion that Paul Bernheim belonged to the impoverished intelligentsia. Still, he invited the diverting young man to the town of D. in the Ruhrgebiet, where the Enders family were based.

Paul was to go to D. in a week's time. He saw that by then he would have to have a job, and not just any job. He should have stuck with Brandeis!

He realised that here was the crunch. He could go to Brandeis, of course. And what then? Pay back the two thousand dollars, and hope the meeting went well. Maybe Brandeis would make him an offer.

For the first time in quite a while, Paul Bernheim got up early. It was a Thursday, his 'lucky day'. Thursdays had always been good to him. All the best things in his life had been on Thursdays. He had taken his final school exams on a Thursday, and he had gone to Oxford on a Thursday.

The sun was shining. Not a cloud in the sky. Not a speck of dust. No wind. The taxis at the stand were all free. He wanted to take a taxi, so as not to waste energy on the jostle in the underground. He climbed in, as though fame and fortune awaited him.

But when he reached the Köpernicker Strasse, and stopped in front of the massive office block which for the last few months had been Brandeis' company headquarters, Paul Bernheim felt afraid, as he had never felt afraid in his life before. If he failed now, he wouldn't even bother to go to D. He thought of what excuse he would make to Irmgard. Writing that note in his head made him feel better. It distracted him from the thought of the next fifteen minutes. The contemplation of his total collapse was still preferable to his fear of it.

He decided not to use the lift, and walked slowly up the steps, counting them as he went. If they came to an even number, then everything would turn out well. When he reached the first floor, the number was odd. He faltered. Luckily there was a board announcing that the chairman's office was on the second floor. Afraid that the number of steps would be odd, he stopped counting.

He had to pass through a large and incredibly sunny open-plan office, with about a hundred desks in it. An office in the American style. Huge electric clocks on each wall, like station clocks. Continuous paper rustle. The quiet chatter of modern typewriters. A whispering, produced by young men poring over columns of figures, writing them down, drawing lines under them with rulers. Bare walls, big bare windows, no curtains. Brandeis liked his visitors to see that office first.

Paul Bernheim prepared himself to be told that Herr Brandeis was in a 'top-level meeting'. He would be kept waiting for an hour or two. So much the better. Time to settle himself.

But within a couple of minutes, he was being taken in to see Brandeis.

Brandeis was sitting in a small, darkened room. Emerging from the intense light outside, visitors could see nothing at all to begin with. He went over to a cupboard, got out a bottle of cognac and two glasses, cigars, cigarettes and matches. These he set down in front of Bernheim, carefully and silently, as though everything – tabletop, bottle, glasses and boxes, even his large, powerful, hairy hands – were made of velvet.

He poured out a couple of glasses.

Bernheim drank his down. He was annoyed that Brandeis only sipped at his.

'I drink very slowly,' said Brandeis.

'I owe you some money,' began Paul.

'The sum is so small it's not even worth mentioning. I must ask for your forgiveness. I meant to visit you. Perhaps you thought I'd purposely avoided meeting you. Not at all. It's become necessary of late to assess and expand the scope of my business. I was occupied with that. I'm glad you came. Only I hope it wasn't to do with that money.'

'No, Herr Brandeis. To be frank: I've come to ask a favour of you.'

'How flattering.'

A long pause followed. Neither man moved. One could hear a bird twittering a long way off. Paul's eyes had become used to the darkness. He could distinguish the dark red of the carpet and the brown of the panelling on the door to his left, a different door from the one he had come through. The darkness was created by shutters outside the windows, which were left open. A gentle breeze blew through the room.

It didn't seem possible to begin speaking again. Brandeis took the bottle and poured more drinks.

'I have lost the greater part of my fortune, of our family fortune,' Paul began again. 'I must look for a job for myself. I have just 25,000 marks left.'

'A sizeable sum – ' said Brandeis. 'But it depends which way you look at it. It could be big or small. For you it's probably small. I could give you some advice what to do with it, if you liked – '

'No, Herr Brandeis, it's too late for that. I need a job within a week, a position, a name.'

Brandeis took another sip. Then he looked into his glass. And, as though he had read the future in it, he asked slowly:

'Are you thinking of getting married?'

Paul nodded.

'Well, Herr Bernheim. I'll see what I can do.'

Paul got up. Brandeis showed him to the door. He held out his hand.

'May one know the lady's name?'

'I'm not engaged yet,' said Paul hesitatingly. He was afraid to take his hand out of Brandeis' soft, warm clasp. 'If you'll promise to be discreet, I'm going to propose to Fräulein Enders.'

'Enders Chemicals?'

'Quite so.'

'I'll be in touch.'

Paul left. Brandeis took one of the cards that lay in piles on his desk, trimmed, rectangular and gleaming like packets of wafers, and wrote on it: 'Enders-Bernheim'.

15

Paul went into a restaurant. He was unable to eat anything. The condition he had been in before going to see Brandeis was becoming permanent. God knows how long it might take Brandeis to reply! The next few days and nights would be hell. He could have used a good friend for these hours, a brother or a mother. Impossible to go back to the flat now. Stay out on the street. Best thing. Wander about like a tramp.

For the first time, Paul Bernheim was aware of the limits of his fortune. He could see himself without a home, drifting steadily closer to the rocky shores of poverty. Up until now he had been surrounded by the boundless ocean of wealth. It was enough for him to see where the limits of his fortune lay for him to see it exhausted. For a few hours he realised that his hopes, his exceptional gifts, his ease and charm, were all the products of the material security in which he had grown up, the fruits of wealth, just like the plants in his father's house. It was as though it had taken the meeting with Irmgard and her uncle, and the possibility of marrying into the chemical industry, to show Paul Bernheim the full measure of bitterness that the possession of a small sum of money is in this world. His 25,000 marks actually seemed to diminish in value, just because they were suddenly made aware of the proximity of the untold sums available to the Enders family. His interview with Brandeis had been humiliating, because Paul Bernheim was one of those people who feel no compunction when asking for love or friendship, for instance, but whose dignity suffers when they have to accept material support. In the scheme of values such people establish at an early age, money counts for more than heart, and more than life. It would be easier for them to accept a life-saving transfusion of blood from someone than a gift or loan of money. Yes, Paul slowly came to hate Brandeis, with that hatred that is a perversion of gratitude.

Paul Bernheim saw his own face among those of the unclaimed dead in the police showcase. He remembered the time he had rashly got himself picked up and taken in by the police. That had been his only encounter with that other, nocturnal world of lawlessness and homelessness. His own future looked at him with the wasted faces of the corpses in the case. As a boy he had sometimes toyed with death, held a knifepoint against his breast, out of vanity and the hope that his death might cause a stir at home, in the town, even in the world. He could imagine his grief-stricken parents, the pious remarks of his teacher at his funeral, the awed discussions among his classmates.

The gush of self-pity he'd felt then overwhelmed him again today. He wanted to mourn himself, and to know himself mourned. A feeling of empathy drove him to seek out the beggars at the street corners and those men who had despair, hunger, homelessness, desolation written in their faces. It didn't cross his mind that each one of them would have counted himself rich and without a care if he'd had just a tenth of Paul's fortune. Paul Bernheim saw no difference between a man stretching out his hand for a coin from a passer-by and a man who, in order to marry a millionairess, had asked Brandeis for a 'social position'.

He would go home. He had the vague idea of making some sort of preparations for some sort of end. He imagined it would be pleasant to take one's revolver out of one's desk drawer, to put one's papers in order, perhaps write a letter, to perform all the ritual last acts that a suicide traditionally did. The cosiness of an hour spent sitting at a desk and taking leave of life appealed to him. An hour whose crepuscular delicacy and melancholy were evocative of winter evenings with no source of light but an open fire.

In the lobby of his apartment building he found a white envelope lying in the mesh letter-box.

He didn't open the letter-box immediately. His debt to melancholy had not been paid yet. He hadn't yet drained his cup of self-imposed agony. But people like him need to exaggerate their misery for a couple of hours, without being interrupted or comforted. It's as though a kind of justice demands compensation from them for the carefree lives they lead; as though Fate gives them their 'crisis' too, so that they might at least become acquainted with an imaginary suffering. Paul Bernheim would have liked to suffer rather longer, to come so close to death that his eventual rescue could only appear the work of providence. This letter – he feared it was his rescue – was too prompt, too simple and too painless. This letter would extinguish his crisis. It was clear to him that by going to Brandeis he had incurred an obligation. His wedding, his future, his whole life – which he didn't doubt would now be great and glorious – he would owe to Brandeis. And perhaps it was out of shame, hurt pride, injured vanity, that he sought refuge in the thought of dying. But vain and proud as he was, he wouldn't really have preferred death to a dependent existence! No! It was enough to experience the mournfulness of a suicidal mood, no more.

But it appears that people of his type aren't even permitted to endure a notional unhappiness. It appears that the guardian angels that cluster round the Bernheims of this world see to it at all times that their charges are kept remote from extremes of pain and joy, that their lives remain in temperate zones of mild winters and cool summers, where the greatest catastrophe is only a passing cloud. Never would Paul Bernheim be deserted by the smiling blessings that had settled over his father, his house, his childhood and youth, his Oxford and his gifts. An easy contentment held him. Never would he escape from the region where one has joys instead of being joyful, endures adversity instead of being wretched, tastes delights instead of being delighted, and in which life is so light because one's self is so empty.

He opened the letter-box. The letter was from Brandeis. To the effect that Brandeis would be happy to welcome Herr Paul Bernheim on to the board of directors of his company. He wants me for the link with Enders, Paul thought. He writes about my valuable qualities, but he has no opinion of me. I'm just a tool for him. Well, I won't!

He didn't go on into his room, and turned away, letter in hand. But by the time he had reached the street, the letter was beginning to take effect. The shadow of death under which Paul Bernheim had crept these past days was dispersed. Paul walked past beggars and derelicts with his usual indifference. They weren't his brothers any more. He went to the lobby of one of the big hotels, as he loved to do. He imagined that this was the only place where a man might be unhappy in style. As he slid into the wide, creaking leather armchair, he was convinced he should reflect, turn Brandeis down, and look for another solution. But when the waiter stood in front of him, Bernheim thought he was beginning to get the upper hand with Fate. And as he ordered a whisky and soda – the confident drink, the drink of the man of the world, and of Anglo-Saxon dynamism – Paul Bernheim felt he had won, as though the waiter's eagerness proved the submissiveness of the world. In this lobby, where the travellers were rich and busy, and had their pockets stuffed with inexhaustible banknotes, Paul thought he recognised his right place. Just half an hour ago he was contemplating suicide. Now he could no longer understand his despair. He had beaten Brandeis. He marvelled at his own adroitness. No one else could have done it, he said to himself, outwitted one of the cleverest men in the world. In his awe at his own performance, Paul didn't hesitate to pay tribute to Brandeis too. He didn't remember the terror he'd felt as he'd climbed the stairs to his office. He didn't remember counting the steps. It no longer occurred to him that Brandeis might be using him. And by the time he took the first sip of his drink, Bernheim had recovered his old bored and arrogant expression, his modern profile, his silken hair swept back, and his fine green eyes fixing the air and a triumphant future.

He had abided his notional death sentence in silence. But to celebrate his notional victory similarly alone was beyond him. He missed Dr König. Dr König had been a charming foil, the perfect listener. But for the last few months he'd disappeared, vanished into the city which he surely hadn't left, but where a man might still lose himself as in the desert sand. Paul Bernheim decided to go and look up Sandor Tekely again. The meeting with him had been fruitful. He went to the Hungarian restaurant.

Tekely's regular place was behind a screen, but facing a mirror that commanded a view of the entrance and the bar. Tekely had originally chosen the place when he was running from his creditors, who didn't scruple to look for him in the restaurant. He stuck to it out of gratitude – he had no more creditors to fear – and out of a superstitious regard of the kind that an American billionaire will sometimes entertain for the places where he once sold newspapers. So Tekely spotted Paul Bernheim the moment he entered. He rose and went up to his visitor. 'May I offer my congratulations?' As though he'd been waiting to ask Bernheim that question for days.

'No, it's still too early.'

'Ah, I understand, you'd rather await Brandeis' reply.'

'Actually, I've got it – ' said Paul Bernheim, and he was sorry he'd gone to Tekely. It was an impertinence of Tekely's to know everything. He didn't allow Bernheim the satisfaction of telling it all at his own pace. Dr König would have behaved differently. And so as to dismiss the debt that he owed Tekely for his part in arranging the recent providential events, Bernheim hastily said:

'If I hadn't run into you – actually I owe it all to you!'

'Oh, you didn't run into me,' replied Tekely, who had anticipated ingratitude, 'you came looking for me! I just wanted to ask you, if you should happen to be speaking to Herr Brandeis about the newspaper – you remember I mentioned it to you – do please mention my name.'

'Yes, of course,' Bernheim assured him, looking up at the clock to pave the way for a speedy escape.

'You must be going,' said Tekely, who knew better than to detain a man in a hurry if one wanted to keep his friendship. 'Don't forget, now!'

'No, no!' said Bernheim, somewhat flustered, and left.

Once more he had the feeling of having been worsted by a stronger opponent, and he began to fear that Tekely might have something on him. He was unhappy, as he always was when he'd been forced to play along in an unpleasant and humiliating scene. How often that had happened to him! Luckily, the only moments his memory recorded faithfully were those in which he had shone; he had the ability to transform embarrassing scenes in such a magically creative way that, after just a few days, they assumed a slightly vague, but fundamentally pleasing appearance. The only terrible experience he was unable to forget was the one in the war with the

Cossack, which kept surfacing whenever his weakness proved itself anew, just as an old wound reopens. Now, too, leaving Tekely, he thought about Nikita. For a moment he had the nightmarish notion that Nikita was destined to reappear in ever-new guises, that he was identical with Tekely, identical with Brandeis, perhaps also with Irmgard's uncle, Herr Enders.

Paul looked for a remedy for this fear. He already knew from experience various remedies against oppressive thoughts, like an invalid who has tried all kinds of cures for a painful condition. He got into a cab, drove home, hastily packed an overnight bag, and went to the station. He congratulated himself on this idea, which saved him from a sleepless night. He was going to see his mother.

Frau Bernheim was startled when she saw her son arriving early in the morning. She was standing in the kitchen supervising the maid, who was cooking breakfast. Paul could remember that when his father had been alive she'd used to take breakfast in bed. She would sit propped up on four pillows under the light-blue canopy and play at being 'Her Majesty'. A broad tray was tucked under her bosom, which was swathed in clouds of lace. In the half-dark room, where the morning light fell through the blinds in narrow stripes, there was a scent of lemons and eau de cologne hovering in the air. The recollection of those morning hours was as heartbreaking as that of some lost paradise. Now his mother was standing in a brown velveteen dressing gown which she could only keep decently closed by folding her arms. Since the war, since she'd begun her economies, she

171

supervised the maid every morning, to make sure she didn't use too much coffee.

'Take another spoonful, Anna, but not a tablespoon, mind!' she called, when Paul came. Amidst her panic at his unexpected arrival, she was also pleased that he hadn't come half an hour later, in which case the gas would have had to be relit.

There were strands of grey hair at her temples, like two rivers of anxiety, or two highways of old age. In the bright light in the kitchen, which received a pitiless cold lustre from the gleaming tiles, Frau Bernheim's face looked crumpled and pale. One might have broken it up into its constituent parts, the strong square chin, the lips, the nose, the cheeks, the forehead. The greying eyebrows seemed to be older than the hair, as though they came from a previous age, and the eyes, where her old beauty still resided like a nervous tenant, lay between puffy little mounds of sleep and tears. His mother's voice seemed high and brittle, she sounded gentler in his memory. It was as though the early morning were responsible for its shrillness, as though it came from the hard gleam of the tiles. The flame on the hob was cold and blue, and burned as if behind glass. Paul couldn't remember ever having been in the kitchen at this hour. It was a revelation. It was as though he had found the source of the wretchedness of the house, and it was the kitchen.

The Defence Ministry widow came down later, much later. She always used a stick in the mornings, as she slowly got used to the movements demanded by the day after the motionlessness of the night. The whole

172

weight of her old body was carried by her stick, her legs only shuffled after supportively. She seemed to Paul like a personification of the sadness that had befallen his father's house. He began to feel afraid of her.

He ate his breakfast quickly, and went into town. He wanted to stay out till the afternoon. He couldn't possibly spend the morning at home. As he walked through the empty streets, tired from his night-long journey, it occurred to him that his mother might die that day. He imagined her dead, and could feel no sorrow. He tried to understand his indifference, and caught himself wishing that his mother were dead. It was impossible to introduce Irmgard to her. Impossible to show Irmgard the house.

He returned late in the afternoon. He told his mother of his engagement, his impending engagement, to Irmgard Enders. 'Enders?' his mother said, and lifted her lorgnon, as though she might be able to read the origin of the Enders family in Paul's face. No, she was not enthusiastic. She knew no Enders.

'They are the richest people in the country, mother,' Paul replied. He appealed to her greed. He misjudged her. What concerned her son was separate, and a different passion was aroused. For the first time in many years, Frau Bernheim could say:

'Money isn't everything, Paul.' He was surprised.

'We're both very happy, mother!' said Paul.

'You can only say that after ten years,' she replied, with a wisdom that was not her own, but that of motherhood.

Paul promised to bring his bride home.

'Yes, bring her, bring her!' said Frau Bernheim.
But he didn't, nor did he later.
Something else happened in the meantime.

16

An amnesty allowed Theodor Bernheim and his friend Gustav to come home.

They arrived in Germany on a grey morning from a bright and sunny Hungary, where spring had already arrived. Nature conspired to make them half-sorry to leave their pleasant exile. Gustav had a ruddy colour, and a quick, healthy, confident air. In returning to Germany he was only doing what was expected of him. Theodor was pale and vehement, his hands fumbled and his glasses were broken. They felt to him not like a broken instrument but like a damaged part of himself. His thin shoulders bore the whole terrible weight of his return to the lost homeland. In such a situation a man, a German, had to be both melancholy and joyful, bitter and mature, optimistic and full of plans. What diverse obligations! From time to time Theodor looked at his travelling companions to see whether he was impressing them at all. 'Of all of our countrymen here with us,' he said to Gustav, 'not one has been through as much as we have. They're returning to their jobs as if nothing had happened, they're just thinking of their paypackets, not one's thinking of Germany.'

'Give it a rest!' replied Gustav.

Theodor shut up. For a very long time, in fact since the day they'd left the country together, he'd been irritated with his comrade. Gustav had made their flight necessary, Gustav had embroiled him in crime and banishment, Gustav had been happy in exile, Gustav was indifferent, Gustav was mindless, Gustav didn't read, you couldn't have a conversation with Gustav, Gustav laughed at him, Gustav had no respect for him. If Theodor had been able to separate his personal feelings from his politics, he would have had to admit that he hated his political ally much more than any of his political foes. But he was compelled to see everything in the light of his wider thinking on Germany and the Jews, the world, Europe, enemies at home and abroad. And so he stuck by Gustav, and was always beginning discussions with Gustav which Gustav would always end with his 'Give it a rest!' If Gustav hadn't been quite a fellow, Theodor said to himself, I would despise him. But since Gustav was a 'fellow', he was forced to admire him.

They said goodbye at the station. That was the frontier of exile. Common beliefs and a shared life abroad were less powerful than the thought of home, which gripped each of them the moment they handed in their tickets. Their home town reached out to them. It was made up of a thousand private, unspecifiable smells, that had nothing to do with politics, nothing to do with nation or race. It was made up of a thousand definite, unspecifiable sounds, which had lived in the memory until now, dissolved in childhood, but which now rose as if in response to the sounds outside. Their home town greeted the returning exiles with one familiar street after another,

176

in which there was nothing public, nothing abstract, no ideal, no politics, no passion, nothing but private recollections. Gustav, the healthier of the two, gave himself up to them, forgot why he'd left home, and why he was now returning. Theodor, though, felt it beneath his dignity to lose himself in private things. He fought the memories, the sounds and the smells. Even now, he was able to perceive himself as a function of something public, his return as a national imperative, his home town as blood-drenched and enslaved soil, and not until he turned into the street where he could see his own house did he become curious to see his mother and the pain that his long absence might have caused her; curious, no more.

She was standing on the threshold to greet him. She had forgotten all the scenes, all the times when worrying over her problem child had made her aggressive and sarcastic. It was her son coming back to her. The hour of his return chimed gently with that of his birth and roused old maternal pangs in her heart and womb. She clasped him to her, without kissing him. Theodor's head rested on his mother's shoulder. Tears welled up in his eyes, his heart pounded, and with teeth clenched and eyes staring behind his broken glasses he strove to retain his 'manly' composure. Emotion wasn't what he wanted now, nor the love of his mother. He would have preferred her welcome to be as frosty as her goodbye had been.

'You've lost weight,' said his mother.

'I'm not surprised,' he replied, not without a hint of reproach in his voice.

'We didn't send you enough money!' wailed his mother.

'Quite,' he agreed.

'My poor child!' she cried.

'No clichés, mother, please! I need a bath.'

'Just tell me, Theodor, how did you live?'

'Like a dog. Vile country, there were coackroaches, it was disgusting!'

'Cockroaches?!' cried Frau Bernheim.

'Yes, and lice too,' added Theodor with relish.

'Heavens! Theodor, you must change out of those clothes at once.'

She went into the kitchen. 'Anna, heat water for a bath. Ten pieces of kindling will be enough, but fetch some more coal from the coal cellar. Here's the key.' Not since the war had Frau Bernheim given the key to the coal cellar to one of the domestics.

She wouldn't leave her son. She accompanied him to the bathroom. She waited for him to get undressed, avid for an opportunity to help him. She was thrilled when she saw that his shirtsleeve was almost torn off at the shoulder. 'I'll sew it up right away,' she said. 'And where are your other shirts?' Lustfully, she waited for her son's nakedness. She was hoping for a physical defect in him, something she might explain as having been caused by his absence from home – like the torn shirtsleeve. Now she beheld her son naked. For the first time since his childhood he was lying beneath her, naked in the water, wearing only his glasses, which he kept on as a last protection, not daring to take them off in front of his mother.

'How thin you are!' exclaimed Frau Bernheim.

'And sick, too!' added her son.

'What's the matter?'

'My heart and my lungs.'

'Were you at least comfortable on the train?'

'There were Jews on it! You can never be amongst your own in Germany!'

'Be sensible, Theodor, leave the Jews alone. That's just something your friends have talked you into.'

After his bath, Theodor went to his room. He had no idea that it had been let. In his shortsightedness, he didn't immediately notice Frau Hammer, who lay wrapped in a shawl on the divan, a short, thin bundle, and uttered a little cry. It sounded like a puppy's cry. 'Who are you?' Theodor asked.

'Get out of my room!' screamed the Defence Ministry widow. Theodor withdrew. He'd only been checking to see what had happened to a pistol he'd left there.

He went to Frau Bernheim. 'I must have my own room back.'

'We have no money, Theodor. It's been let for a year.'

'I must have my room back!' he repeated.

'Please behave, Theodor,' his mother begged him.

All at once she collapsed into an armchair, covered her face with her hands, and began sobbing silently. Theodor watched her shoulders shaking. An unknown force pulled him towards her. He took a step forward, and stopped.

I mustn't weaken! he said to himself, and: Women always cry in their old age. He turned on his heel, walked over to the window, and looked out at the garden.

Suddenly he turned and asked: 'Where am I going to sleep?'

'Anna will sleep in the kitchen, and you can sleep in the room the coachman used to have.'

'I see,' said Theodor. 'You'd never put Paul in the coachman's room. I'm sorry I ever came home. But you wait! Just you wait!'

In the afternoon he went to Gustav's.

Gustav was sitting in the midst of his family, his married sisters, his three brothers who were all postmen. There was a smell of celebratory sauerkraut and of freshly roasted coffee beans. The post office had offered to take Gustav on. Within a week, Gustav would have a job. 'He's finished with politics,' said one of the three postmen. The three of them were sitting with their uniform jackets unbuttoned. Their caps hung on hooks by the door like triplets.

'After a year he'll be able to go to university. He'll save. We'll all save,' said another of the postmen.

'Our father always steered clear of politics too,' observed the third.

'We don't want anything to do with politics,' said Gustav's mother, looking fixedly at Theodor.

Theodor grasped that he was not popular with his friend's family. Every word that was said to him had a hostile undertone that he couldn't decipher but that worried him. These little people behaved as though Theodor had been Gustav's political adviser. And now Gustav was sitting in the midst of his brothers and sisters, and was suddenly one of them, and was unpolitical. The celebratory smell from the kitchen embraced them all equally, and gave them all a cheap, cosy and evident pleasure. Theodor realised that he had lost his political associate. Gustav no longer had any political views. He was set on making his way as a decent, honest bourgeois.

'Miserable race,' thought Theodor, sniffing with his thin, blunt nose. He quickly said goodbye.

When he was outside again he felt his solitude – which had always seemed weightless to him – was suddenly oppressive, like a heavy body.

I will work hard, learn and understand, he resolved. Gustav can be a postman if he likes.

At home his mother showed him a short letter from Paul. In a couple of sentences that read like an official communication, Paul announced his engagement to Irmgard Enders.

'He got lucky,' said Theodor.

'Let's hope so!' said his mother.

'Ambitious,' muttered Theodor.

Frau Bernheim left the room. Theodor had not been back more than eight hours, but she was already suffering from his return. It was like an old curse. Theodor had come back like a rheumatic pain that she hadn't felt for a couple of months and had forgotten. Oh, she knew her son. He'd always been like that, and always would be.

She gave him a key to the front door and told him he could come and go as he pleased. He could eat in his room. Lunch would be left for him. She raised her lorgnon briefly. Her eyes sealed what she had decreed. And from now on she only saw Theodor by chance, when their paths happened to cross.

It was only weeks later, a few days before Paul's

wedding, which was to take place in Berlin, that Theodor spoke to his mother again. He asked when she would be going. She replied: 'I'm not. A poor mother wouldn't look good.'

'But I'm going,' said Theodor.

'I thought you didn't like your brother?'

'It's a chance to make contacts.'

Frau Bernheim reflected for a few seconds. Then, in a surprisingly sharp voice – the one she used on the porter – she said: 'I'll write Paul a letter. He'll send you some money, and you'll go to Berlin and stay there. I can't have you here any longer. You need a few contacts. It's time you started earning a living. Get your things packed.'

For the first time, Theodor felt respect for his mother. She stood before him, a little taller than he was, but old and worn, her left hand on her hip, and her right pointing away down the corridor, where his suitcases were. She was throwing her son out of the house. No question.

Theodor went to Berlin. He went to Paul's hotel and had himself announced. Paul asked him to wait in the lobby. Theodor regarded this as a snub, and considered going away again. All right, he said, very well. I will live on the streets and starve. Very well! But he lacked the strength to leave the lobby. It was a grand hotel. That fellow isn't letting me upstairs, he thought, to stop me from seeing that he's living in a suite of rooms. Very well. Each 'very well' he whispered to himself consoled him a little, as though it meant something, or constituted some revenge.

Finally Paul came down. 'Very natty,' said Theodor by

way of greeting. They shook fingertips, and sat down in silence.

'What will you drink?' asked Paul unhappily.

'No camomile tea, anyway!'

'Whisky?'

'All right.'

'Listen, Theodor,' Paul began. 'When we're back from our honeymoon, you can visit me once a month on a set day of your choosing. Now, here's my solicitor's address. For six months you can draw 500 marks a month. By six weeks from tomorrow, you have to have found a job. Here's the address of my tailor. Get yourself three suits made. You can come to the wedding. It'll be here, not in church.'

A long pause ensued. They sipped at their whisky and sodas.

Then Theodor got up, shook a loose bundle of his brother's fingers, and left.

He went straight to the solicitor.

There he was told, 'Your brother asks you to call on Herr Brandeis on the morning of the day after tomorrow. Herr Brandeis will be expecting you.' He was given his 500 marks.

Paul's wedding took place the next day. It passed off smoothly, quietly and speedily. Theodor barely had a chance to look at Paul's wife. He saw Brandeis among the five male guests.

'That's the fellow who's buying up half of Germany.'

In the lobby, Theodor watched as Brandeis immediately detached himself from the other guests, and walked off with a surprisingly light step for a man of his size.

'I'd rather not be around him too much!' remarked one of the guests in Theodor's vicinity to another.

'Yes, he's one of those people who've made it on the back of the Inflation,' replied the other.

Theodor knew that one of them was Herr Enders. The other might have been his twin. Both seemed to be made of a smooth, hard substance, and they were reminiscent of planed wooden bowling-balls. Their voices were so loud they could be heard all over the lobby.

'Those people,' remarked Herr Enders, and stopped by a pillar, as though to prepare himself for a long and fatiguing exposition, 'those people are as different from us as pirates from ordinary seamen. Pirates is what they are!'

'Absolutely right, Herr Enders. Whereas our fathers made their fortunes by the sweat of their brows, these people have made money unscrupulously and by sheer luck. That's the difference. And notice that most of these piratical types have come from the east. No morals, I say.'

'I'm glad he's got Bernheim on his board at least. But that's about the only crumb of comfort.'

'I still wouldn't care to deal with him,' said Herr Enders' *Doppelgänger* to Herr Enders.

'But you'd be wrong,' replied Herr Enders, who always covered all the angles. 'Doing business with someone is different. If we show people of Brandeis' type how a proper businessman behaves, or a real industrialist, then we'll be making honest men of them.'

The two of them moved off. Theodor remained behind the pillar. The conversation had filled him with confidence, and a feeling of indebtedness to Herr Enders. He had felt such resistance about going to Brandeis and

184

thanking him! But now that he understood what good society thought of the Mongol, his interview with Brandeis was much simplified. Far from him being my benefactor, he thought, it's Germany that's been good to him.

Thus armed, Theodor went to see Brandeis the next day. He didn't walk up the stairs as his brother Paul had done, he took the lift. But while Brandeis had seen Paul Bernheim right away, he kept Theodor waiting for a long time. The waiting room was bare and white, and specialist magazines of no interest to Theodor lay around. Theodor began walking up and down in his agitation, and tired himself out. The fellow's trying to humiliate me, he thought, but I'll teach him! He kept walking back and forth in the empty room. His stride grew ever heavier, his weak eyes could see nothing but the misty, oily white of the walls. He took out a pocket mirror, examined his pale, peaked face, and was satisfied. He thought he looked wise, distinguished and resolute. He pushed out his lower lip, to give himself a more dynamic profile. His thin neck puffed out. With his fingers he checked the parting in his pale blond hair. At that moment he was summoned to Brandeis.

Brandeis rose so slowly that, by the time he was on his feet, Theodor had reached the desk. He then rather tumbled into the soft armchair, whose depth he had misjudged in the darkness. Brandeis took just as long to sit down again as he had to stand up. He waited. Theodor couldn't get a word out. It was quiet. Somewhere, a clock ticked. Brandeis kept his heavy, hairy hands on the tabletop.

185

Finally Theodor got up. 'I have to thank you!'

'You don't have to do any such thing,' replied Brandeis, remaining seated. 'Your brother told me of your wish to see me. I understand it wasn't your wish at all. It was his. He thought you should work for me.'

'For you?' asked Theodor.

'I can't say I agree with the idea myself,' said Brandeis. 'I don't think you'd be right for us. Besides, your political views are disruptive, really very disruptive.'

'I'm a conservative and a nationalist.'

'Those are words,' said Brandeis very softly. 'I would describe myself as conservative, and you as extremely radical. I hardly think it's conservative to go around in a brown shirt, shouting and demonstrating. It isn't, shall we say, well-bred.'

'You have no right to pass judgements on that.'

'You mean I only have the duty to help you!' said Brandeis quietly.

Theodor sat down again. He saw Brandeis very close up, his gaze wandered over the steppes of his yellow face. He had to admit he now thought similarly of demonstrations and brown shirts. He recalled Gustav's family. Suddenly he thought it might be better to get in with Brandeis. Easy enough! he thought. And he leaned forward and said: 'I happened to catch a conversation of which you were the subject, Herr Brandeis.'

'And you want to report it to me?'

'Yes.'

'I'm afraid I have to disappoint you. I'm not interested. I know that people who have been rich for twenty years think of me as a pirate because I've only been rich for one.

Perhaps,' Brandeis smiled, 'perhaps they also think I'm dangerous – they're afraid of me,' he suddenly finished, almost shouting.

Then, in his usual soft voice, he resumed: 'I think you have the makings of a journalist. Now, I could recommend you to a right-wing paper. But there are several of your sort there already. On the other hand, you might be an acquisition for a democratic paper, an old paper of great tradition, whose publishers are under an obligation to me. A young man with an extreme right-wing background like yourself might be useful to a democratic paper. Or, to put it another way: you can work for the Jews. How would you like that?' Theodor wanted to say yes, but Brandeis didn't wait. 'Let me know.' He got up. Theodor left silently, and with a bow that he immediately regretted, because he thought it had been a little too low.

Part Three

17

At seven o'clock in the evening, Nikolai Brandeis left his enormous office block, two hours later than his staff. Five o'clock was closing time for his three department stores and his thirty-three shops, and their 650 employees put on their coats, looked out their season tickets, their sweethearts and their peevish wives, and went out to the cinema, the theatre or the cut-price concert, the commissionaires and drivers went into pubs and raised thin glasses full of frothing urine-yellow liquid to their drooping moustaches. It was the hour that five thousand workers poured out of the factories whose shares Brandeis held, into damp halls full of cold pipesmoke, and the mouldy smell of beer barrels and sour sweat, to listen to politics. It was the hour when secretaries and white-collar workers went to the casino for a round of cards, to the Stahlhelm association, to the committee of the White Cross, to the local branch of the Reichsbanner, or the Kreiszahlstelle's weekly meeting. At this time the drivers of Brandeis' fleet of 120 vans and lorries took off their uniforms, hung them up on spindly coathangers in numbered lockers, and put on their cheap, functional mufti, ready to make the most of their liberty, which lasted for barely twelve hours. It was the hour in which the editors of the democratic newspaper – whose shares Brandeis secretly owned – began their night's work, putting on green eyeshades, and pressed white rubber bell-pushes. Messengers arrived on bicycles with parliamentary reports and court reports, with the news of the day in purple ink on cheap pulpy paper; with political correspondents' reports; and then the telephones would start ringing in the stuffy leather-upholstered telephone booths, from Amsterdam and Rotterdam, from Bucharest and Budapest, from Calcutta and from Leningrad, and the leader writer had found his subject, and was walking back and forth dictating sentences, which a typewriter gave back to him in a rattle. All these people imagined they were free. They barely knew the man who gave them their bread and margarine or finest dairy butter. They had a confident air, but were afraid of getting the sack, they demonstrated on Sundays and hid pornographic postcards from their wives, they shouted at their children and worried about whether they would get their pay rise, they dictated leaders and tipped their hats to the editor.

Brandeis they didn't know. Nikolai Brandeis, the organiser, the creator of the new middle class, and the preserver of the old one, Nikolai Brandeis who gave discounts to middle-class organisations, who grew rich from the low prices of his goods, who clothed men and fed them, who lent them small sums of money and pretty little houses on the outskirts of town, who gave them flowerpots and twittering canaries and their liberty, their twelve hours of liberty.

At seven o'clock Nikolai Brandeis left his office,

together with his first secretary, Colonel Meister. That evening, just before leaving, Brandeis had suddenly begun talking. To begin with, the colonel had understood precious little. He had similar experiences when he happened to pick up a book. At first the words would just swim in front of his eyes. Then he would try to currycomb them out, and look at them one by one. And then he would be surprised to find that it was possible to understand the words, but not their meanings. When Brandeis started speaking, he rather suspected that what he was hearing was what he called 'philosophising'. Only much later did he begin to understand; and then not with his everyday mind, but with the help of instincts whose existence he had never previously guessed at.

'Now,' Brandeis said, 'I'm almost there. Anyone else in my position would say so. But I don't have just one life behind me, I have two or more. And for some time now I've had the feeling that it's time to start on yet another one.

'Do you believe me if I say I'm tired? Not from working too hard, but from working without appetite, without ambition, without a goal. Today I can still wield the power my company has acquired, but tomorrow I'll be its slave. Did you ever wonder why I've become so rich? You think it's because I'm a great businessman? You're wrong, Colonel! I owe everything to the supineness of people and institutions. Nothing nowadays puts up any resistance. If you want a throne, a country will come forward, begging you to be its ruler. Launch a revolution, and you'll find the proletariat ready to give up their lives for it. Start a war, and you'll find nations just waiting to take up arms against each other. Within a few weeks or months, perhaps a year, I might be able to control the whole of German industry. I've realised that it's only the names that frighten people off, with their established and powerful sound. You hear about a company chairman and you go to call on him – and when you do you feel a fool, and that your preparations have been a waste of time. His title's on a brass plate on the door, but once you're inside his office, you see that all the power of this chairman is kept in place by four screws and a bit of brass, and the door and the brass and the screws are far more impressive than the man they represent. Believe me, the chairman is a function of his nameplate, his business cards, his job, the fear he inspires, the salaries he pays, the sackings he carries out – not the other way round! I'm already in danger of that myself. Soon the trappings of my power will start to be more impressive than I am. I'll no longer be able to indulge the whims that now are my only pleasure. I can put Herr Bernheim on the board, if I like, and watch him grow, watch him marry into the chemical industry, get a big house and a big name for himself. I'm happy to have his brother, a nationalist, writing articles for a Jewish newspaper. But tomorrow the newspaper could have more power than I'd care for it to have. For instance, it might unmask my anonymity. The moment my name is spoken, the way the household names of the powerful are spoken, I'll be powerless. Because my name will grow and draw strength from me, and require my strength to make noise – mere noise . . .

'And yet – and this is why I'm speaking to you – I'm tempted by chemistry, the only mystery in all the transparency I inhabit. I'm in danger of losing myself to it. And for the first time I would be in the grip of something stronger than myself. Everything else was lesser than I: that absurd middle class that provides me with my slogans and packs my stores, the employees I provide with clothing and bread and houses, the bank with its small secure loans, my directors, with their 150,000 mark salaries. But chemistry is *elemental*. I might become just as helpless as its shareholders, its chemists and its chairmen. Ever since I've been in touch with the Imperial Chemical Industry, the astonishing phenomena in the world of chemistry have terrified me. To me, it's all entirely miraculous. Other figures don't impress me. But I'm terrified by the 10,000 employees of Höchst am Main, the 11,000 at Baden Aniline, the 95 factories of I.G., the 108,000 workers, the 143,000 in subsidiary plants, the 600 tonnes of phosgene produced annually. Did you know that the rayon of your daughter's stockings is related to poison gas? Both are nitroglycerine. What a name! Nitroglycerine!

'Do you think I'm raving, Colonel? You're right! I've begun to rave. Something has changed, something has happened to Nikolai Brandeis. I don't know how many more times we'll leave this office together. Goodnight.'

He didn't understand, thought Brandeis. I didn't tell him all of it, either. I could talk for days without getting on to what really matters. I've started being overwhelmed by strange forces. Since then –

He didn't go on. He often reached that frontier. Beyond it lay a wide terrain, unknown and unexplored, accessible to no thought and no imagining. It was the

195

edge of the world towards which Brandeis had once travelled.

His steps slowed as he approached his house.

Yes. As he approached his house, his steps slowed. How many times he forgot it in the course of a day! It was one of the many houses he had acquired. Sometimes he slept in a hotel. He loved strange hotel rooms, their anonymous fittings, and their wallpaper that chance had glued on. All he needed was a roof over his head. But in his house, wealth proliferated like a disease. A gardener, a couple of dogs, a garage, servants, a creaking gate and crunchy gravel. And the foundations embedded deep in foreign soil, concrete with roots. He would have liked to live in a tent. Many things belonged to him, but he owned nothing. Many people obeyed him, but there was no one whom he might command. Many things yielded to him, but none of them was his property. It was as though his houses were only the paper plans of architects; the goods he bought and sold only receipts and invoices; the people who worked for him just the alphabetical lists of their names. Once upon a time, he had owned three fields, a small cottage painted blue and white, a few cows, two horses, a dozen books, a rifle and a metal-tipped cane. All that was gone! And now, as though he had acquired nothing since then, Nikolai Brandeis lived like one dispossessed, contented and inspired by his poverty. He thought it was his destiny to flit like a shadow through a world of property and concrete, with a ghost's mysterious ability to acquire fortunes, mindlessly shuffling banknotes with his hands rather as one's feet rustled through leaves in autumn, and in general converting everything – objects, merchandise and human beings – into paper. Owning nothing, and not being owned either! It was for others to obtain and to cherish, to inherit and to keep, to prize and to enjoy, to buy and to possess. Or was the property of others perhaps not real either? Only they wouldn't admit it? They thought they held it in their hands, but it trickled through their fingers? They thought they enjoyed it, but it vanished? Their enjoyment, like their feeling of ownership, a phantom of their imagination? What I told the colonel was true, thought Brandeis. Everything is unresisting and collapses into ashes and sand before the force of my will. Only the names still exist. There is only one actual force which grows, which brings life and death: chemistry. Should I abandon myself to it?

At home Lydia was waiting for him. Lydia had been waiting for him for more than a year, in vain. He shared his bed with her, and held her in his arms, and his gaze, which shone in the darkness when she opened her eyes in the continually disappointed hope of catching him with his eyes closed, his face finally lost in rapture. But it was never other than it was in the daytime. Yes, it seemed to her as though it actually had more clarity in the dark. Perhaps she would one day find the secret of this man at such a time, the way the identity of a ghost is revealed at midnight. She waited in vain. His eyes seemed able to see the distance into which he shortly wanted to disappear. Colossal though he was, so heavy-footed that even the carpets echoed under him and she heard the gravel crunch in the garden, he was still remote and unfamiliar to her. Sometimes he would cup her breasts in his great hands. A powerful warmth flowed into her body from his fingertips. He didn't speak. 'Don't be so silent,' she would beg him – in the vague hope that he might be silent in some other way. That he might one day speak like any normal person she scarcely thought possible.

He made her at once happy and unhappy, as though the two conditions were inseparable twins. She could no longer tell whether he was tender or cruel, or whether her own love might not in fact be curiosity or fear. For minutes at a time she would hate his remoteness and long for the simple, coarse humanity of Grigori. She decided many times to leave him and go back to the Green Swan, but she kept putting it off. Unless he's different in two weeks, I'll leave him, she would say to herself. He didn't change, and she stayed. Her modest imagination, formed by the modest insights of novelists into the souls of men, sometimes suggested one of the remedies that novels prescribe. She began to consider the pathetic alternatives. Could she make him jealous, perhaps? From the scant experience of her past love-life, she tried to devise recipes, make up situations, use the ancient tricks of literary tradition, which life imitates so wonderfully well. But one look at his face was enough to tell her how laughable her endeavours were. No laws could apply to him. He never raised his voice so that it might be heard in another room, say. She was sometimes unable to feel his presence even when he was visibly there in front of her. His great heavy body lay on her, her teeth bit at his mighty neck, her fingers pressed against his granite shoulderblades, his breath caught in her hair. She would lie covered by him and forget that he wasn't a man like others. A sudden longing made her open her eyes and look up at him. She saw the whites of his eyes. What was Brandeis searching for in the wall above her head? Could he see through walls? Could he see the horizon of his homeland? At such a moment, a deadly hatred ignited in her. She could have stabbed him, to see if he was mortal.

She was imprisoned in her house. He allowed dress-makers and tradesmen to come to her, but not a single visitor. He didn't want to see anyone. People were like houses and merchandise to him. He traded with them during the day, in his office. She counted her years. She was still young. Twenty-two. She reproached him with the figure, as if her youth were his fault. Once he saw her crying. He understood. But he sat, powerful and clumsy, before the small unhappiness of the little woman. He was afraid of his own pity. He distrusted the ability to comfort. He was not able to see unhappiness in terms of the person who felt it. He never grasped that while the thing causing a hurt might be slight, neither its extent nor its depth need be. He measured Lydia's unhappiness by the absolute unhappiness of the world. He looked on indifferently as she wept. It was the first time she had wept before an indifferent man. It was, she thought, the first humiliation she had suffered in her life. Her little brain schemed revenge. She started having moods. She tried to exercise a little despotism. She surprised Brandeis with unexpected wishes. She asked to see people. He took her to the theatre one evening. Silently, not without bitterness. The foyer was bad enough. He dreaded the first act. To him the play was like a looming catastrophe. The directors had toned down the experimentation of the

199

first post-war years, the radicalism of dramaturgy had begun to make concessions to the conservatism of the audience. Brandeis' fear was replaced by an even more dangerous apathy. He had appeared with Lydia a few times in theatre boxes, at balls and concerts. Then he had stopped bothering about conventional social engagements, which the new age continued to practise, even in the abeyance of a society. It was enough for him to confirm, every few months or so, that he had indeed lost all interest in the goings-on on stage. That evening, his indifference to them was so great that he began to watch the audience. He realised that more people knew him than he thought. His anonymity was under threat. People can't bear to live without their devils and their saints, he thought. They find me inscrutable. I've had enough of appearing to those fools as a kind of eastern demon. Let those rich Jews take over, the ones from Kichinev, Odessa and Riga, the ones who want more than anything in the world to be native Berliners. Seeing them like that, rows of faces, blank physiognomies like skulls, as if shaped by barbers who worked not only with hair, beards and moustaches, but also with noses and mouths and foreheads – he realised for the first time that he had been driven to make money by a single passion, one stronger than all her sisters: the passion of contempt. Contempt can take hold of a man, just like love or hate or gambling. A 'mortal contempt' is possible. It had taken these rows of illuminated faces to make Brandeis aware of his passion, just as the sight of a person may make one aware of one's love for them. So many people he didn't know, all greeting him. They knew he didn't know them. And still they smiled imploringly up at him. They had the obtrusive submissiveness of people collecting money for public charities, people who hold out their hands and are afraid of being taken for beggars. The interval came. They trod a circle in the hall outside, afraid of slipping on the polished floor. Between the unease of their feet, in new boots with smooth soles, and the feeling of distinction they derived from the National Theatre, the ushers' uniforms and their own dinner jackets, there was an empty space which their bodies tried vainly to fill. But they fell away between their gratified expressions and their slipping feet. Like a rotating frame, they spun round the empty, mirroring oval of the middle of the floor, where no one walked for fear of being alone. Brandeis remembered the Sunday he had watched the march on the Kurfürstendamm. There too the centre had been left vacant. They were the same faces that were now circling during the interval. The brown shirts had been left at home. Only the arms were different. They didn't swing now. They drooped down on either side of the dinner jackets, like stiff black artificial limbs. The ladies' colourful evening dresses reflected on the white faces of the men, like the colour play of a socially acceptable sexual act. Everyone felt he was at a première. Everyone was glad everyone else was there too. Because it was only together that they made up the colourful scene for the reporters on the first night.

Brandeis missed his youngest director Paul Bernheim, and his brother Theodor. To Brandeis' mind, the colourful scene would have been enhanced by the presence of Paul and his young wife. The only other person of his

201

acquaintance he could see there was the theatre critic on the democratic newspaper he controlled. But the critic hardly knew his employer, it's only the financial editors who are really informed. Art renders the people involved in it innocuous. Perhaps Paul Bernheim didn't attend premières these days, his social position would no longer permit it. I'll ask him round, thought Brandeis. I'll introduce him to Lydia. With any luck, he'll fall in love with her.

Young Frau Bernheim had gone to stay with her uncle Enders for a fortnight. A small family celebration, nothing of any significance. Paul Bernheim had discharged his obligation with a day's visit. This was the first time he had set foot in Brandeis' house. The first time he had seen the woman Brandeis lived with. He came with his head full of the rumours that were being spread about the Caucasian princess, rumours which he believed. Because, in an age where truths are scarce, nothing is so credible as rumour, and the more far-fetched it sounds, the more gratefully it is received by romance-hungry imaginations.

Paul Bernheim was among the most credulous recipients of novelettish rumours. He collected them, as he collected jokes, in a gold-embossed, leather-bound notebook which he would secretly consult before telling them. He kept a clear distinction in his mind between so-called stories and the so-called truth. But it pleased him when a story intruded into the reality surrounding him. Like most Europeans, who have a literary sense of geography, he thought the east was mysterious and the west ordinary. The east began at Katowice, and extended as far as Rabindranath Tagore. This was the region where he placed Brandeis. Lydia was even further east. Because she was a woman, and, according to what Tekely said, from the Caucasus, and probably of noble blood too. The Caucasus would have been enough on its own.

A man doesn't love a woman, but the world she represents for him. Although Lydia had a European face, and might just as easily have been born in London or Paris or Cologne – in fact she was from Kiev – Paul Bernheim saw her as 'the Caucasian type', and since he had no idea of her past in the Green Swan, he quickly classified her as an authentic lady, exotic and distinguished. He would make such deft formulations in order to satisfy his need to see himself as a connoisseur of women and the world. Even as he characterised the woman for himself, he could already hear himself talking about her, and to the regard he had for the Caucasus he added that which his imagined listeners had for him. He was so overjoyed at the appearance of this story in the midst of his reality that he elaborated the one and neglected the other. He was the type of man who transforms himself in the presence of a woman he might one day care to seduce. He produced his old charmer's qualities, and started to tell stories about Oxford, which never failed in their effect on men and women alike. He was the first man other than her husband to talk to Lydia for more than a year. She compared the massive, taciturn Nikolai Brandeis with the animated and loquacious Paul Bernheim. There were even a few moments in the course of the evening when a secret alliance seemed to be forged between her and Paul, against Brandeis. When Paul remarked: 'So, you don't entertain much?' she replied very quickly: 'Never!' So quickly that it suggested she'd been expecting the question.

Thereupon Brandeis remarked softly: 'I don't care for strangers.'

'What about you, madam?' asked Paul. She gave no reply. Nikolai Brandeis was staring fixedly at the table, but he also took in the walls, which were in shadow, and the two people with him. The hard, alert light of his eyes flooded the whole room. Typically, he was gripping two corners of the table, suggesting that he was just about to get up. But Paul sometimes wondered whether Brandeis wasn't about to push the table over instead. He felt very clearly that he hated Brandeis; perhaps it had just taken the woman to crystallise his feelings. His initial feeling was envy. That Mongol, Paul said to himself – unconsciously borrowing his brother Theodor's terminology – possesses her every night. For naturally he saw sex as a confirmation that the man possesses and the woman is possessed. That man, driven by nothing but avarice, behaves like an eastern potentate, and shuts her up in his harem. Of course he's jealous. Why wouldn't he be, in my presence? Paul was able to forget the awkward fact that he owed his career to Brandeis. He was paid a salary of 150,000 marks, for which he worked three hours a day, and performed representative duties. The meetings he had with insurance companies and shop stewards were beneath him anyway. He suspected Brandeis of deliberately keeping a man as dangerous as himself away from the 'foreign service', specifically from negotiations with banks, when banks were Paul's speciality. He was annoyed that Brandeis had helped Theodor so quickly and deftly. He almost envied his brother his job on the paper. He was just waiting for an important job himself. What harm would it have done Brandeis to make Paul Bernheim one of the exalted managing directors of his publishing firm? He's scared of me, Paul consoled himself, while his own fear of Brandeis awoke like an old pain. In the murky distance was the terrible memory of Nikita Bezborodko. He didn't yet admit it to himself, but he was looking for the weak point in his enemy's life. He thought his being invited to the house – 'breaking into it', he called it – was due to his own cunning. Of course Brandeis had a 'weak point'. It was this woman. Paul's psychological faculties had been nurtured by novels in which a rich, powerful man vainly seeks the love of a beautiful woman, only to lose her to his skilful rival, a man with a profound understanding of the female psyche. He could already see things moving that way. On this terrain, if on no other, he had the beating of Brandeis. This was where he would get his revenge. But as he was too sentimental to avenge himself without some moral alibi, he deemed it necessary to fall in love with Lydia. So he fell in love with her.

He suggested taking them both out for a drive the next day, expecting Brandeis to refuse. But Brandeis accepted.

The following day, though, Brandeis made his excuses. He asked Bernheim to take Lydia on her own. They drove at 70 kilometres per hour, a speed which is recommended for such situations by modern authors who have studied the connections between the human heart and the internal combustion engine. Paul, who since his marriage had taken up contemporary literature again, and had even met some contemporary writers, was an expert in the improved access to natural beauty made possible by speed. 'I need to drive like this at least every other day,' he told Lydia. 'It's only the invention of the automobile that's taught us to appreciate nature fully. It's wonderful, the way roads and trees and houses are gobbled up. My driver's a coward. He never does more than 55 or 60. But to my way of thinking, a man who works fast needs to relax fast. We're at risk all day anyway, just sitting in the office. Believe me: I couldn't live without danger.'

'Were you in the war?'

'In the cavalry, four years.'

'You love riding, too?'

'I go out once or twice a week. Would you care to come with me?'

'I'm a bit scared.'

'Not in my company, surely. We'll find a nice quiet mount for you.' Memories awakened in Lydia Markovna of a series of photographs called 'The Horsewoman', which had appeared in a 'leading' fashion journal, in shimmering blue-green on glossy paper, alongside another series called 'Mother and Child', and a third, 'Society Couples'. She saw the captions under the pictures: 'Frau Generaldirektor Blumenstein', or 'Countess of Hanau-Lichtenstern on horseback', or 'Morning Gallop', or 'Gentleman-Riders'. And all the symbols of social distinction – which, because of the shortage of living material, had transplanted themselves to photographic images, to the editorial offices of illustrated newspapers and the studios of film companies – now awoke in Lydia's mind, and made her socially ambitious. Show me the watchmaker's daughter from Kiev who wouldn't have yielded to such temptations. Her father had been a watchmaker, but she had always felt herself destined for something better, and the poems of Pushkin, in conjunction with an unremarkable dramatic gift, were to help her reach it. In the same summer that Nikolai Brandeis deserted from the Red Army, Lydia's father died. She fled. She became a waitress in a Russian restaurant, where she refused tips, and thus – and because the diners' imaginations required examples of the brutality of the Revolution – she acquired the reputation of being a noblewoman. It was in this restaurant that some émigrés, former actors, founded the Green Swan. They took Lydia on. So, by a roundabout way, her wish came true. It wasn't exactly the Moscow Arts, but it was a theatre. Since all her colleagues had paired off, and only she and Grigori the Cossack slept alone, eventually, after some hesitation, she moved in with him. It saved the company the expense of an extra hotel room. When she left with Brandeis, she had hopes of a spectacular rise. But instead of reaching the charmed circles of the 'grand monde', as she'd hoped, she became a girl in love with a silent, remote and incomprehensible master. She was jealous of the long days that Brandeis spent away from home, she didn't know where. He had forbidden her to seek him out in the daytime. She wondered if she dared ask Paul. Did Brandeis have other women? She sometimes dreamed she was only one of a number of women he kept locked up in a number of houses. Would he be jealous? 'I hope Herr Brandeis isn't inclined to jealousy!' Paul said suddenly, with the quiet, probing scorn the professional seducer uses for his absent rival.

'No,' she said.

'I should be if I were him!'

Lydia was grateful to him. Women believe whatever assurances they happen to need. For centuries they have been seduced by lies rather than the truth. She had never had a compliment from Brandeis. She quickly asked: 'What about your wife?' and immediately regretted it.

'My wife?' asked Paul in perplexity, as though he'd entirely forgotten he had one. 'Oh, yes, you must meet her some time.'

She decided to ask Brandeis whether Frau Bernheim was pretty, petite, statuesque, blonde or dark. She would have no peace until, as well as knowing the man, she also knew about the woman who belonged to him, or apparently belonged to him.

Because the evening was getting chilly, they drove slowly back into town. 'Do you dance?' asked Paul, thinking of the most orthodox way of approaching the body of a woman.

'Oh,' she said innocently, and with no thought of the consequences, 'not since the Green Swan!'

'The Greeen Swan?'

'It's the name of a cabaret.'

'So?'

'I acted in it.'

His astonishment was boundless. It could hardly have been greater if someone had told him that his wife wasn't a born Enders. Nothing so troubles a man like Bernheim as to learn that the woman in his car with him is not a princess but a former actress. 'Oh!' he said. And, as at the fancy dress ball he had suddenly lost the ability to pursue his caressing of Fräulein Irmgard Enders, so, conversely, he now lost the ability to keep his distance from Lydia. His knee pressed automatically against her leg. He forgot to speak. He stopped the car and, without saying a word, tried to put his arm around her.

She realised what he was trying to do, and, a couple of seconds later, what prompted him to do it. She felt the same mute and desperate shame she had felt when Grigori had sold her to Brandeis. But today she couldn't even manage a cry. It was as though her heart had become used to accepting humiliation. This was no new indignity, but the repetition of one suffered previously. Not out of desperation, but more out of an instinctive attempt at self-defence, she started sobbing quietly. Tears are the only weapon of the defenceless.

It took Paul several long minutes to realise that he had offended Lydia. As his mother would endow, say, a civil servant with a different sense of honour from a private tutor, so her son would not permit an actress to feel as offended as a Caucasian princess, let alone a born Enders from the Rhineland. But while chance occasionally proved his mother wrong, his own doctrine of varying honour among different classes of women was evidence of a particularly profound ignorance, which he shared with his fellow-seducers. For there is really nothing that is so independent of class, of family, of occupation and education as a woman's understanding of her own honour. Princesses and prostitutes are demeaned and flattered by the same things. When Paul realised why his

209

companion was crying, he felt sorry, because he was a decent sort – and he also regretted the 'muffed opportunity', as men in his social bracket are wont to say. He stopped. Without looking at him, her face lowered, Lydia got out of the car. She walked straight ahead, not looking where she was going. He got out and followed her. He spoke, but she didn't hear him. Shame roared in her ears. At last he realised there was nothing to be done. Then his concern turned instead to his Packard, which he had left in the middle of the road. He turned back, drove into a side road, and was left with the awful feeling of having suffered a defeat.

Sentimentality is the sister of crudeness. And nothing could be more in the natural order of things than that Paul thought ruefully and lovingly of Lydia all the way home. She seemed more desirable to him, and more precious, by virtue of the fact that he had conclusively lost her.

At home his eye lit on an enlarged photograph of his wife. He found Irmgard dull and unappealing. Sport had made her mannish, her shoulders were a couple of centimetres too broad, her hands were large, dry and strong. Lydia was gentle and soft, her skin had an ivory smoothness, her nipples were probably brown moons. A shudder ran down his spine.

Lydia waited a long time for Brandeis. He arrived late, towards midnight. He saw her reddened eyes, asked no questions, and went away again.

It was one of those nights he intended to spend in an anonymous hotel room somewhere.

18

All the roads in the world look alike. All the people in the world look alike. Sons look like their fathers. And whoever has understood these things must wonder at the impossibility of change. Yes, however much fashions change, and forms of government, and taste and style, the more clearly they show the old eternal laws at work everywhere, the laws by which the rich build houses and the poor huts, by which the rich wear clothes and the poor rags, and also those other laws by which the rich love like the poor, are born in the same way, sicken and die in the same way, pray and hope, despair and wither away.

We will now consider the house of the prosperous Paul Bernheim, and for this it is not unimportant to remember the house of his father. Old Bernheim had the trees felled and the walls knocked down, while his son had a wall built, and old, mature trees planted in the virgin soil of his plot of ground. He had no dwarfs in his garden. Then again, Grützer & Co. were no longer producing them. Instead, they had turned to making female figures of a rather spiky quality out of thin, milky, hollow porcelain. Their limbs were like pine needles. Their breasts were little pyramids, their bellies parallelograms, their elbows lances, and their thrice-bent knees were reminiscent of medical models showing the effects of rickets.

There were some half-dozen such figures in Bernheim's hall. They were gifts from Herr Carl Enders, and provided evidence of his progressive tastes, or rather of his efforts to prove that he had such tastes. Without question, he would really have preferred the clay dwarfs that had graced old Bernheim's garden. But he would only have smiled at them pityingly. Carl Enders' criterion for buying a picture was that it should repel his senses and his intelligence. Only then could he be sure of having bought a valuable modern work. Long years of practice had brought him to the stage that he would be automatically impressed by anything he disliked, and would react to anything he liked with indignant suspicion. It was by such a method that he had secured his reputation of having 'an infallible eye'. And so he went on, in the teeth of his own natural taste. The villa where Paul lived, its furnishings and the works of art in it, were all a testimony to Herr Enders. The house resembled a ship without a keel. Only the windows, which reached down to the ground, so that one might go in and out through them, suggested that it might be a dwelling. Otherwise, it was painted white all over and seemed to be steaming along. A semi-circular redoubt, inside which one could – or should – eat breakfast in summer, seemed from the outside to contain the first-class cabins. The roof over the redoubt was like a spacious ship's bridge. The first floor was not as high, and its windows were more modest. They were shaded by a protruding flat stone roof. Above that there was only an attic, a wide circle with low walls and lateral slits of windows with no function other than to fly flags from when the occasion demanded. The grounds were extensive. The few transplanted trees clustered round the house, as though afraid of the barren expanse of the garden. Of the three elements of 'light, air and sunshine' that were sacred to Herr Enders and to modern architecture in general, Bernheim's house seemed at times to have more than the whole world, and one often had the impression when it was overcast outside and the air was a thick mist, that the rooms were full of their own private sunshine. Paul's favourite place was by the fireside. This feature, once the principal amenity of human dwellings, has degenerated to being merely symbolic in the residences of the well-to-do, a place to divest oneself of the day's rigours. Paul Bernheim's hearth was topped by a stone pyramid, on whose broad rim there was space for a glass of water, a cigarette case, a box of coloured matches and a blue vase of geraniums. It had a brass fireguard, and was surrounded by a black-and-white stone chessboard, which made an island across the wooden floor. There was a floral-patterned armchair to the right of it, and an upholstered stool to the left. A steel erection that might have supported a camera, or equally hats, coats and umbrellas, surprisingly terminated instead in a green lampshade, in whose thickly padded interior an electric bulb flowered. Paul opened the door through to the dining room. He loved to sit by the fireside, looking towards the soft light of the dining room, where broad white chairs with gently supporting straw seats were grouped around a bridally veiled table, in the middle of which was a white bowl

213

full of yellow flowers. A gong in a nickel frame might easily have been taken for a shaving mirror. Only a timely glance at its grey rubber-headed hammer preserved the unwary from falling into error. The whole house was amazingly clean and new. Paul Bernheim never sat down on a chair without first inspecting it, out of a general wariness of wet polish. There was a permanent smell of varnish and oil and turpentine – a smell that Irmgard combatted every morning with an artificial scent of pine needles. The pictures would be draped to protect them from the spray. Only in Irmgard's bedroom was there a different smell, one of cold cream, lipstick and curling-irons. Facing her broad bed was an exclusive picture by the exclusive artist Hartmann, who had sold it to Herr Enders for 50,000 marks. Herr Enders resented paying artists, tailors and barbers, because he thought of them as providing a public service, like clean streets and lighting, for which he paid his rates, and had given the painter a cheque for only 10,000 marks, in the vague hope that time would reduce the balance. In his opinion there was nothing that could resist time. It devoured men, things and debts. It was particularly menacing to the artist Hartmann who, as he grew older, became an ever easier prey to women who would take him to the edge of the grave, and then leave him there. Herr Enders was constantly predicting the painter's suicide, not least because he was still owed his 40,000 marks. The prospect of his death, of course, only added to the value of the picture. Irmgard could see it from her bed. During the day it faced the windows, where it had good light. For the night-time, Herr Enders had devised a special arrangement. A narrow frame of matt glass would light up at the flick of a switch that was placed over the bed. Thus Irmgard could take the picture – itself a prefabricated dream – into her dreams with her.

Paul Bernheim sat down in front of the fire. But today it didn't soothe him. He was alone in his crackling, new, varnished house, although he could never feel at home there, because he was continually reminded of the overwhelming power of Herr Enders and the chemical industry. Where could he feel happy? At work it was Brandeis who oppressed him, at home Enders. Ah! He had imagined he would have an easier time of it. He had imagined that within five months he would have become a force in the great industry. But the industrialist Enders was even cagier and more duplicitous than the financier Brandeis. Paul had the strong conviction that he was being kept in reserve, like an unused tool. He had been left to lie in a drawer, like a hammer which one of them might one day use to bang in a couple of nails. His experience with Lydia wasn't the only thing upsetting him. Though he was one of Brandeis' directors, he had only discovered indirectly that Brandeis had secretly started buying up shares in the Transleithian Corporation. Moreover – and this too he had had to find out for himself – a lumber company had been set up in Albania under Brandeis' aegis. What was Brandeis up to in Albania? There was talk of him building railways there in partnership with the Italian government, but that he was refusing to purchase the materials in Rome. Now the Italian government was trying to insist on that as a precondition for giving him the contract. Gradually

Bernheim discovered the purpose of the journeys Brandeis was going on every other month. His destination was the Balkans, but he only had his mail forwarded as far as Vienna. He's getting dangerous, thought Bernheim. When he started making his discreet purchases, no one knew him. He was left to get on with it. 'Not now, they won't stand for it,' he muttered to the roaring fire. Just then the telephone purred. It would be Irmgard, who called every evening.

'How are you?'

'How are you!'

'Everything fine?'

'Everything fine!'

'Say something loving!'

'Irmchen,' he mumbled. He couldn't possibly speak endearments down the telephone. Irmgard always insisted that he did, just as she always liked to ask about the servants, chauffeurs and linen.

'Have you heard?'

'What?'

'Uncle's buying me a horse!'

'Terrific!' cried Paul, with simulated delight that almost died in his throat.

'He wants a word with you now.'

Then it was Herr Enders. His voice sounded very far away, because he never spoke into the mouthpiece, just into the general air. A servant might use the telephone while he was out of the house, and leave his germs on the mouthpiece. Every month he replaced all the telephones in the house. 'My dear boy,' said the faint voice, 'what news of Brandeis?'

216

'You tell me.'

'Trans- and Cis- Inc. Queering our pitch. Rayon in Eastern Europe.'

'Could be,' said Paul.

'Find out. Irmgard'll be back the day after tomorrow. *Pupille!*' This last was a word that Enders liked to append to confidential telephone conversations, a kind of acoustic seal.

Paul returned to the fireside. He could hear Herr Enders saying to Irmgard at this very moment, 'Don't take it amiss, but that husband of yours is a fool.' The words were rather more audible to him than what he had managed to hear on the telephone. Should he go and visit Brandeis? What would he learn there? What if Lydia had talked? What a scandal! His reputation as a gentleman!

The word started off a new chain of associations. The dreams he'd had before he got married. Independence, chemicals, market domination, stock exchanges, deals with America, aeroplane flights, London and Paris for two days, New York on the third, a worldwide network of power, controlling interests in every German newspaper. At home, a life of parties, tennis, riding, boxing. Not the boring people who came now. Not those morning exercises on the wireless that Irmgard was so addicted to. No, he hadn't become powerful. No one respected him. His life as a bachelor had had more dignity and freedom. Relatively speaking, Theodor had come on faster than he had.

Paul went over to the gramophone – another gift from Herr Enders – and put on the recording of the five King brothers from Wilmington. The sound of their deep, soft voices deepened his melancholy to the desired point, at which it became comforting. He moved his chair closer to the box, so that he could keep winding it up. He couldn't stand the silence in the house any more. Those Negroes had to keep on singing. They sang the despair of an entire race, and included the despairing listener in their own hot and agonising past. Paul sent a look of heartfelt gratitude towards the gramophone, the only one of Herr Enders' presents that he had any use for. Twenty years ago, he would have had to sit down at the piano himself. Now you simply cranked a handle. The technology of consolation made progress, but progress still allowed sentimentality.

He asked for the newspapers, and opened them at the home news page. Not without guilt. He told himself that as a businessman he should look first at the financial page, but the urge was stronger than he was, and he looked up the exhibition notices, theatre reviews and family tragedies. The day had its share of disasters, and the newspaper carried an article by his brother Theodor, about an exhibition devoted to bookbinding, but also about Germany, Europe, the yellow peril and India, because Theodor never missed an opportunity. He always had to voice an opinion, and had a panoply of meaningless but impressive-sounding phrases at his fingertips. He had picked them up, taken them apart, reassembled them, and filled them with elements of populist thought, of Marxism and Max Stirner. Paul went to the trouble of getting up, going over to the fireplace, and feeding the newspaper to the flames. He was one of those sensitive people for whom, once a thing is out of sight, it no longer exists.

The Negroes were still singing. The fire slowly died. Paul Bernheim didn't switch the light on. He dropped off on the patterned armchair, whose large yellow flowers bloomed toxically in the dark.

19

Theodor was putting on his dinner jacket. His face beamed back at him from the mirror in all its festive pallor. With a pair of nail-scissors he tried to clip a few hairs that were growing out of various places in his ears. When it came to his appearance, he was all painstaking care. He took another look at his slender hands. They were proof of his aristocratic descent, and he was proud of them. Then he got into his dinner jacket, tugged at the lapels, and turned all the lights on. Technical rehearsal. He tried to catch himself in profile, by turning the wardrobe mirror till it was at an oblique angle to the large wall-mirror. Then he took off his glasses, and for a moment his mind was blank, as though the absence of visual stimulus had cut off any thoughts he might have. He heard the typewriter rattling next door. A secretary was busy copying his latest article. He listened to the galloping keys as though they were music. 'Now she'll be on page three, the bit where I talk about the unconsciousness of the night in our German cities. "Unconsciousness of the night" is wonderful.' After that, the secretary had some letters to type. 'The correspondence,' Theodor said. Whenever he got a lot of mail, he felt himself moving closer to the epicentre of the world. Each time a reader wrote in with a response to one of his articles, he would straightaway show it to his editors, so they might value their contributor at his true worth. And he showed it to his friends, in particular those among them who might be annoyed by it. He answered every letter he got. He applied for invitations to parties, exhibitions, conferences, and the pseudo-salons of bank managers, of a general, of a minister. The following day he would report what he had said there. His aim was to show 'those fellows' a new type of 'young German', sober but patriotic, aristocratically bred but progressive, diplomatic in his thinking but outspoken. In fact he was constantly petrified lest he had said too much. He was reluctant to antagonise certain 'fellows', even though he hated them. These included his publishers, magazine editors, and the sub-editors who worked on his articles. If one of them wrote a piece himself, he would get a phone call from Theodor right away: 'Congratulations! Marvellous piece!' To his friends, though, he would say: 'Did you see that article? The fellow has a nice style, but he's so naive. Just can't see the world for what it is!'

The rattling stopped. His secretary knocked on the door. Although Theodor didn't think it proper to have a human relationship with his secretary, and saw her merely as 'personnel', and not as a woman, he did quickly slick his hair down with his fingers before calling 'Enter!' He sat down at his desk to read the typescript. His secretary stood next to him. He got to the place about 'the unconsciousness of the night', quickly turned his head to her, and said, 'Good, eh?' Immediately he was angry with himself. He could never find the proper mean between his hunger for praise and the need to keep personnel at a respectful distance. Occasionally, he would even forget himself to the extent of reading aloud to her an article which was very topical, and which there was no time to type out. The poor girl, who typed business letters from eight to four every day, felt that her job with Theodor was a daily bath in wit and style. She worshipped him. She read the books he reviewed in the light of his comments on them. When Theodor became aware of her adoration, he reduced the distance between them by a couple of centimetres by saying to her, 'Are you tired? All right, then we won't do quite so much today!'

He put the typescript in an envelope and wrote 'Urgent!' on it, although it wasn't actually urgent. But he loved giving things a prod and hurrying them along. Nothing that wasn't pressing could be important. Speed, speed. Out of contempt for the normal passage of time, he set his watch a little fast. He consulted it now. And though he still had an hour, he said: 'Right, I've got no more time now. You can go!' She left. He sat down, turned the handle of his gramophone, and listened to his recording of the King brothers from Wilmington. The music of those Negroes set him up nicely. He was going to a party, and meant to 'show those fellows'. He was going to his brother Paul's house, of all places.

Yes, there was a French writer expected at Paul Bernheim's house. He was one of those writers who, after the war, worked to improve relations between France and Germany, a kind of literary dove of peace. The taxes they paid on their royalties were spent by the Minister of War on preparations for a new war. At the same time, the

Minister of Culture sent these authors with recommend-ations to the German Embassy in Paris. Thereupon various groups for mutual understanding, reconciliation and culture invited those authors whose books had been translated to give talks. The writers came, gave their talks, were invited back to private houses, were fed truffles, and benevolently studied the mores of their erstwhile foes. They made notes for proposed series of articles on German poets, German company directors and German revolutionaries. Attended by German pro-fessors of French as by archangels, they visited the houses of the wealthy, the cultured and pan-European, the industrialists who produced poison gas in their factories and read Keyserling at home.

The writer hadn't arrived yet. Professor Hamerling had, though, and thought he could detect the silent reproaches that were forming in Paul Bernheim's mind. Frau Irmgard's questions: 'Does he know his way around Berlin? Did you give him the correct address, Professor? He hasn't been given the wrong invitation, has he, Professor?' rang like accusations in Professor Hamer-ling's ears. The other guests arrived, one after another. The illumination in the room seemed to grow ever brighter with the light of peace that each guest carried before him like a lantern. They nodded, they missed the names of the people they had been introduced to, and they beamed into each other's faces – not with their eyes, but with their shining teeth. People felt exalted in Paul Bernheim's house, which was one of the most modern in Berlin. Everything *comme il faut*, people said, using French expressions for social topics, just as Latin is used in medical conversations. Paul Bernheim had – *comme il faut* – invited people from all camps. Herr von Marlow was there with his wife, a Junker, and a man who had moved from the German Nationalist to the Populist Party since leasing his property in Silesia and moving to Berlin. The asphalt of the city was turning him into a liberal. The ideal of *bon ton*, which had previously been to act as nationalistically as possible, now favoured taking a European view of things. Every year Herr von Marlow would send the Emperor at Doorn his best wishes as a loyal subject on His Majesty's birthday – in a roundabout way, and so that only his closest intimates got to hear of it. This wasn't a political expression, but rather a private ritual – just as the Berlin Jews, long since lapsed, go on celebrating their holiest festivals in a kind of shamefaced secrecy, but Christmas publicly, and for all to see.

The editor of a democratic newspaper came, who, starting seven years ago from a radical position, was now – like Herr von Marlow, but from the opposite direction – moving towards the centre ground, ever since his wife's large dowry had enabled him to acquire a small estate in Brandenburg and, thanks to his contact with the soil, a set of more right-wing opinions. Even though his wife bought clothes in Paris every season, she still betrayed her commercial background. But she was forgiven, in the hope that her regular riding lessons in the Tiergarten might ultimately transform her into a properly feudal country lady. With her olive complexion, she wore a dark green dress and brown make-up. Frau Irmgard was wearing an almost identical model, but in her own colour, blue, the result of a trip to Paris undertaken at

224

much the same time. I'll just have to order my next dress in Vienna, thought the editor's wife. Then she looked at Frau Irmgard and saw with a shock that she had probably just had exactly the same thought. She does have rather thick arms, though, thought the editor's wife. She does have rather thin arms, though, thought Frau Irmgard at the same time.

The celebrated journalist Freytag came with his wife, whose dresses came rather less expensive than her husband's articles. The glances of the richer ladies met briefly and significantly, and Frau Freytag went down in flames. Her dress actually came from one of the sales that the big stores hold at the end of the season to sell off those items that have been worn once or twice by models. Frau Freytag had hard features, and the wrinkles round her eyes, though she was still young, only thirty-six, showed that she had never had a facial. But the early years of her marriage, when her husband had been what is called 'a little scribbler', now seemed belatedly to have etched themselves into her face. The traces of worry had come gradually, and long after the events, like faintness after a surge of adrenalin. Frau Freytag was unsure of herself when shaking hands. Her elbow was clamped by her side, and there was something awkward about her hand – it suggested a hand held out in a kitchen, recently wiped on a blue apron. There was a major from the War Ministry, wearing civilian clothes apparently held up by whale-bone, with a hard ornithological face, and beady eyes like boot buttons. From left and right, people met in the middle, and formed groups in their discomfiture. Individuals leaving these groups suddenly looked completely lost, and felt a need to rest against something. Their shoulders shyly tested the solidity of the fixtures. A brilliantly illuminated sadness and lifelessness hung in the air. Frau Irmgard was at pains to speak to all her guests individually, *comme il faut*. She was relieved whenever someone had to apologise for his wife's last-minute indisposition, because that paved the way for the little variation: 'Oh, I'm so sorry to hear about your wife . . . ' That required no thought, and was always appropriate.

Eventually the French pacifist arrived, somewhat dazzled by the gloomy festivities in his honour, and still not used to the ways of this foreign race. They wouldn't have seemed quite so strange to him had he not come with the firm intention of writing about them. That intention, in turn, demanded that he find interesting things to notice, where things were only ordinary. Coming from a nation that finds all it requires within its own boundaries, and thus rarely crosses them, Monsieur Antoine Charronoux loved to pursue the remarkable in foreign countries. His visit had a literary purpose, and he was required to find material, whether it was there or not. He rushed from one impression to the next, and jotted them all down in a similar rush. His decision to write about the country quite automatically – as it were on behalf of his future readers – cast a romantic light on the people and objects he encountered, and each one proposed itself as typical. Monsieur Charronoux was delighted when he heard Professor Hamerling describe himself as a francophile. Henceforth all francophiles would bear Professor Hamerling's countenance. The professor was just then in a far corner of the room, holding forth on his chosen subject to Messrs. von Marlow and Freytag. 'What they have,' he said of the French, 'is that sober, practical good sense which we Teutons so conspicuously lack, with our souls forever shrouded in mists. What I admire more than anything about the French is their cheerful *savoir-vivre*, their way of eating and drinking and making love. Paris is the capital of common sense and sensual pleasure. We remain Nordic, and our element is the pearly twilight of a Northern evening.'

'They need us, we don't need them,' said Theodor, who had just arrived. With his instinct for serious and controversial debate, he had automatically made straight for the group around Professor Hamerling. Everyone looked at him. He had a thrilling sense of his own youthful energy as he confronted the eminent professor. He thought he could hear an admiring gasp from the others. 'Paris,' Theodor went on, 'has long since ceased to be a centre, as Berlin is and will be even more in future.'

'That wasn't what we were talking about,' said Hamerling crossly. 'French *légèreté* has its home in Paris. Berlin works, Germany works.' Monsieur Charronoux was just approaching the group. He caught the last few words, and decided to quote them. He was impressed by such clear and memorable remarks: for days, without realising it, he had been the eyes and ears of his future readers. 'Paris is the home of lightness, and Germany of work.' What a pregnant formula. Future war was out of the question!

At table, he sat next to Frau Irmgard. Everything *comme il faut*. She had long since decided that she would show him round the house and the pictures. She was wondering if it was appropriate to take him to the bedroom, where the great Hartmann was hanging. Tentatively, she broached the subject. 'Unfortunately, it's in my bedroom,' she said. Monsieur Charronoux shot her a glance, a new sort of glance, as though he had just put on spectacles. He could visualise this bedroom, and it might be of interest to see how this social class slept. A man at the French Embassy had assured him that there were more separate bedrooms in Germany than anywhere else in the world. Perhaps a short chapter on sexual mores was in order?

In the midst of his guests, Paul Bernheim felt an utter stranger. He looked round at all the women. Why wasn't Lydia there? He didn't love her. He said it again. No, he didn't love her. 'Desire' came to mind. That was the word. He desired her. She had taught him that he wasn't irresistible, that in fact he was clumsy and crude. A childish feeling came over him. He wanted to lie on the floor and kick and shout 'I want to, I want to,' as he had done when he was a boy. 'I want Lydia, I want Lydia,' he murmured quickly, ten times over, helplessly and mechanically. Each repetition hurt. He could follow the path of every word. It seemed to come from his heart, run through his veins to his brain, stay there a while, and then back to his heart. I – want – Lydia! What torment!

He waited for the end of the meal, as though something decisive would happen then. Something impossible. All the infinity of time ahead of him, a whole lifetime, echoing with this unfulfilled desire. It had to be hacked up, chopped into pieces, and some decision reached about each piece. His hopelessness was easier to bear that way than as a single, enormous, all-encompassing whole.

228

A multitude of disappointments, one at the end of each fragment of time, was better than one single one.

People rose. In a flash he decided to go out. Brandeis' villa was just round the block. It was as though he had only just realised this, and Lydia's wonderful proximity came as a last possible solution. It simply wasn't possible to be so close and to stay apart. He ran out into the street. He turned left, then left again.

He saw the two dazzling eyes of a car in front of Brandeis' villa. The gate and the front door were both open. Two men in uniform, obviously the chauffeur and the doorman, carried out a couple of large suitcases and put them in the back of the car.

Paul stood in the shadows. He heard voices. He was hot. His hands couldn't grip. He felt for the railing to lean against. He heard Lydia's voice, like distant singing. He couldn't understand what she was saying.

A few seconds later, Lydia left the house. The motor was running. It was a soothing sound for Paul to hear. As long as it's warming up, there's time, he thought. The noise softened the intolerable glare of the headlights. Paul measured the short distance to the car. It would take him a second, no more, to get to the door handle. Another, mobile Paul Bernheim detached himself from the first, leapt over to the car, got in and drove off. It had only just happened, and yet it seemed years and years ago. All at once, everything was over. His adventures and ambitions, social position, power and love and the world, all lay in the past. It was as though everything he did and thought and felt was just repetition for form's sake. Someone had given him the part to play because he had once lived it and was well versed in it.

Suddenly the revving of the engine stopped, and the headlights veered round and bathed him in light. Paul Bernheim lowered his head. It was over in a second. The car slipped by him in silence.

Finally he let go of the railing. He was going. It was as though he had been standing there for twenty years. The front door of the villa was still open. Golden, consoling light shone from the hall. Brandeis stepped outside.

His eye caught the shadow by the railing. 'Who is it?' asked Brandeis.

'Me,' replied Paul.

Brandeis went up to him with the light, noiseless tread that was so at variance with his bulk. It was as though he borrowed a different pair of feet to walk with.

'Did you want to see us?'

'No,' said Paul, 'I wanted to see her.'

'Lydia Markovna has left for good. She's gone back to her theatre. They're in Geneva now. Go if you want.'

'No,' said Paul. And he thought: My father would have gone, my father would have gone.

'We can say goodbye now too,' said Brandeis. 'I'll walk you back to your house. I'm leaving tomorrow. I may not be back. I don't have the ability to stay in one place for a long time.

'Actually, I owe you an apology. It occurred to me a few times to measure myself against the element your marriage has brought you closer to. I wanted to save you for later. I never had much respect for you, or for people in general. My opinion doesn't matter. I should have told you in a letter, but since I've found you here, I'm telling you like this, though I find the circumstances a bit absurd.'

'I don't hold anything against you,' said Paul. 'Just now, even five minutes ago, I should have been deeply offended. But now I feel old. Look at my hair, Herr Brandeis! Hasn't it gone white? For the last three minutes I've had the impression that I was a young man when I left my house, and I'm old now. I think I'm wise enough to admit to you that I've always admired you. Admired you, and feared you too. But I'm still not sufficiently wise not to ask you: Why did you despise me?'

'I'm not sure,' Brandeis replied. 'Your weakness. For instance, you wouldn't have been able to leave everything a day, or even an hour, before reaching your goal, as I'm doing now. It doesn't require strength to conquer something. Everything yields to you, everything's rotten. Leaving it, leaving it is the thing. Even so, I don't have the feeling I'm doing anything extraordinary. Something tells me to move on. Just as something else made me come in the first place. It tells me to move on, and I obey. Good luck, Herr Paul Bernheim. Try, perhaps now you'll be successful.'

They had reached Bernheim's house. All the windows were lit up. Paul thought he could hear his guests' voices. He felt in his pocket for the key. And as he took it out he said casually, as though it concerned the front door: 'Tell me, Herr Brandeis, did you send Lydia away?'

'No, she left. I don't send people away. She left, and perhaps that's why I'm leaving too. I don't know what keeps me in a place, or what makes me leave it.'

There was silence.

231

Then Brandeis said: 'Goodnight!' And without await-ing an answer, he disappeared into the shadow of the trees that lined the road.

20

Some days later, Nikolai Brandeis left a train at one of the frontier stations he had so often passed through previously without ever having seen more of them than the barren, limitless sadness of the shunting yards, the provisional aspect of the creosoted brown sheds, and the similarities between the uniforms of the customs officials of the two countries. He stayed in the little border town which he reached after a half-hour walk from the station, as though this stay – and his finally giving in to a wish he had fleetingly and frequently had – was proof of his re-acquired freedom. The little town's quiet inhabitants turned to stare at him. His face seemed made from the same stuff as his brown overcoat, and although his suit and hat and shoes were of European cut, on him they looked like garments worn by a foreign tribe in some remote and inaccessible land. Brandeis walked slowly through the small, narrow streets, which seemed to grow even smaller and narrower when he appeared in them. A great emptiness formed in front of him and behind him.

As yet, he didn't know where he would go. The earth seemed to him to be the same all over. In every country, in every city, with infinitely patient and painful bounty, it gave birth to the weak Paul Bernheims, the prisoners of their misguided wishes; the miserably confused Theodors, living in the eternal shadow of public pathos; the strong men whose power turned to weakness, and who suffocated in the poison gas they produced; the ordinary citizens, who came from Budapest and sat behind glass partitions; and the little girls who wanted love, and lost their little hearts.

Let the world go its eternal boring way, but without me, thought Brandeis. Paul Bernheim will eventually get into the chemical industry. Herr Enders will come to the rescue of the Fatherland in the next war, Theodor will write leaders in the papers whose shares I own. Where shall I go? All the world's ports are waiting for me.

At about six o'clock in the evening he boarded another train. At the same time, old Frau Bernheim's ivory knitting needles started to click, and so did the typewriter in the house of her son Theodor. Frau Irmgard saw out the family doctor, and got ready to tell her husband the usual joyful tidings. She was carrying a child. Herr Sandor Tekely went to the Hungarian restaurant in the Augsburgerstrasse. The drivers of Brandeis' fleet of trucks took off their company uniforms and put on their cheap suits. The officials rang their girls, and pulled cut-price theatre tickets from their wallets. Work began on the morning papers. The editors put on their eyeshades and sharpened their red pencils. And the news jingled its way into the leather-upholstered telephone booths, from Bucharest and Budapest, from Amsterdam and Rotterdam, from London and Bombay, from Cairo and New York. The world was going its boring old way.

Brandeis was never seen again. Since that day, there has been no information of his whereabouts.

He boarded the train, and another Nikolai Brandeis was born.

It was the beginning of a new chapter.

For further information about Granta Books
and a full list of titles, please write to us at

Granta Books

2/3 HANOVER YARD

NOEL ROAD

LONDON

N1 8BE

enclosing a stamped, addressed envelope

───────────────

You can visit our website at

http://www.granta.com